To Greg Heitz, who opened my eyes to the profession of testing, and who opened his own to proofread this book.

Valentin

I dedicate this book to my Mom who made me applied where I never thought I would study,

to Charlène who encouraged and supported me during this adventure,

to Capucine and Charlie who accompanied the writing of this book with their children's games.

Henri

THE MISSING LINK

VALENTIN GUERLESQUIN

HENRI BIGOT

Dogma

1

....

For several weeks now, Louis has been working on setting up a testing strategy for his new project: the introduction of automated testing as part of a major initiative. This audacious initiative chosen by the Company combined regulatory issues, obsolescence of existing systems and substantial financial gains linked to operating savings. Consequently, he found himself facing some serious challenges.

Each week, one of the consulting firms hired by his employer presented him with the progress of their mandate. Their reports were of little interest: a lot of time spent on comparative tables of automated testing tools, a few tips on how to organize tests in an agile context. In short, content accessible on the Internet. It was not inspiring.

Culturally, the Company was used to planning everything. The IT department liked procedures and saw in ITIL the guarantee of delivering the right product at the right cost, sometimes even on time.

A group dedicated to application testing, the Test Office, had produced many procedures, document templates, and other test-related artefacts. Good employees were the ones who followed protocols, filled out all documents, and made sure that those documents were approved by just about everyone in the Company.

However, the Company had been promoting agility for some years. Acting quickly, eliminating unnecessary interactions, giving priority to the necessary over the superfluous: these were the guiding principles. The stated objective was clear: to be able to deliver software faster to the business line, always with a concern for quality.

It was 5:30 pm when Louis arrived in front of Denis' office. Since that morning, he had been searching for the answer to a seemingly simple question the project manager asked about his initiative: what will be the cost of testing, and more specifically, the cost for automated tests? His project manager wanted to evaluate the return on investment…

Denis' mission was to make automated testing a reality within the Company. To achieve this goal, he worked with his team to introduce different models, and to change the traditional approaches to testing that were deeply rooted within the organization.

Upon entering Denis' office, Louis was embarrassed. He had been working in software testing groups for a few years, yet he had never been involved in automated testing. He had heard about it, of course, but he had never had the opportunity to practice. Moreover, Louis did not consider himself a great technician. His domain was rather teams organization.

"Do you have an idea of the scope of your initiative?" asked Denis. "Do you already have epics defined, or an idea of functionalities that will be delivered?"

"Not really, since it's much too early in the project. We know that we're going to start by delivering to the Company's Asia office, but I must admit that for the moment I don't really know what that means."

"So how do you expect to know how much it will cost to test?" exclaimed Denis.

"You know how it is," replied Louis, annoyed, "we have to do the test strategy document, and that includes the cost estimate"

"It's not agile," Denis replied dryly.

"We will! We're planning to deliver in an agile way!"

"No, that's not what I'm telling you. It's not agile to want to estimate the costs of the functionalities for the entire initiative from the outset."

Louis was facing a fairly common problem. Large organizations using a traditional approach to deliver their software, the "agile shift", did not always have the necessary change in mindset in how to deliver it. Project managers, converted to Scrum Masters, adopted the Sprints rhythm and its jargon, but still wanted to plan costs, deadlines, and resources for the entire product in advance.

A few days earlier, for another initiative, Denis had seen a former project manager, promoted to the rank of Product Owner, present the delivery plan for a new product for the next eighteen months. Everything was there: Sprints, the content, the weight of each of User Stories, all Release dates. All of this he had done on his own, as the development team had not yet been trained. Denis and his colleagues in charge of transforming practices were dismayed. Yet the rest of the audience seemed satisfied: proof that agility and Scrum could be structured and predictive!

"How many people will be working on this initiative, and for how long? "asked Denis.
"It's a multi-year thing. The product will have to be deployed on every continent. So there's really no end date."

"And the team, do you have any idea how big will be?"

"Maybe fifty or so…"

"Fifty developers? Wow! That's a lot," exclaimed Denis.

"No no, there will be about twenty developers. Several squads, groups of four or five. In the fifty people, I include Project Managers, Scrum Masters, Product Owners, managers, analysts... everyone!"

"Ok. But tell me, does five testers for twenty developers seem plausible to you? Do you think they'll be able to test the product as it's delivered?"

"Probably," began Louis...

"Instead, you should first talk to the project manager about capacity and build a team that you will have to train in test automation. If you feel that five is enough to test the product, ask for a total of ten testers."

"Double that?" exclaimed Louis. "But why double what we think is needed? I'm going to have a hard time defending that!"

"Because you might lose some on the way. Not all of them will be able to be effective in automated testing, or else they won't like it. Let's say that it concerns fifty percent of your team, so that will leave you with five automated testers, in the end, the number of testers will be in line with the size you have imagined."

"Yes, but I'll have too many people afterwards to do tests, whether manual or automated."

Denis had never had the opportunity to explain to Louis his dogmatic approach to automated testing. Their various meetings had always taken place in the presence of the supplier of part of the solution, or the consulting company, or both. These situations were not conducive to a frank discussion. Today it was finally possible.

"In fact," Denis began, "you don't want to do manual testing. You don't have to. Consider that your strategy relies entirely on automated testing. Your group is going to have to test everything that is necessary and sufficient to gain confidence in the product, and this in an automated way.

In a strategy like this one, you leave no room for manual testing. Out. You don't want it. But let's agree, we're talking about the strategy, about what you're going to propose as an approach. We know, you and I, that that's not going to happen... At least not at first... But by affirming it, by sharing it and by getting management to admit it, you set the scene. You're going to make it clear: automated testing is not an option but the heart of our testing strategy.

At the beginning, you will have to train your team. They'll suck. And yes! You're certainly not going to be able to automate the appropriate tests for what is going to be delivered by developers. And that's perfectly normal.

With ten testers, for example, you'll be able to do only a fifth of scripts needed for each sprint. So that's eighty percent of the rest you'll have to keep running manually. That's also why, at the beginning, your team has to be bigger than necessary."

Denis knew the team would do less at first. He estimated the count would probably be two to five percent. But there was no reason to discourage Louis right away. Twenty percent was a round number, easy to use for his demonstration.

"Now, let's assume that all your testers successfully convert themselves to automation testers. By that, I mean that everyone might like it and eventually have the qualities required to become automated test developers. That would be good news, because you'd end up with five extra people. A lot of managers in the organization will be happy that you've already trained them: all managers have been instructed to introduce automated testing in their teams, but they can't find anybody on the job market.

And then as your team matures, those who don't get hooked will always have a place as manual testers, whether on this initiative or elsewhere."

"And how do you choose which tests to automate, and which to keep in manual testing?" Louis asked.

"You didn't listen to what I just said. You have to consider that absolutely all tests have to be automated. That's Dogma! Consider those that aren't as abnormal. Doing these tests manually will be the penance of your team! That's a bit like how believers atone for their sins, isn't it? That's why I call it a Dogma."

"Okay, I get it. It's the posture that's important. That we share the target and do everything we can to reach it. I guess as we sprint we're going to learn, get more comfortable, be more efficient, and gradually get to the one hundred percent. But my question remains unanswered: which ones do we automate first, since we won't be able to do everything at the beginning?"

"If you were experienced, I would tell you to start with the ones that are the most complicated to do manually, the ones that are most likely to find defects. But then again, if you were experienced in automated testing, you might not be here to stop me from going home... So I'm going to suggest something else: start with simple tests, with tests that speak to everyone. First of all, because the whole team will understand them, but also because it will reassure everyone. That's what most people expect from automated tests - to do things with low added value for a human. By showing them at the beginning what they expect to see, it will help you to continue, and to get the support of management. The key is to get started. Then, your objective will be to constantly progress. But you will probably never reach one hundred percent."

"Why not?"

"For different reasons. Let's just say that some aspects may not be automatable. But you won't choose. You can't know which ones and how many today, so keep that one hundred percent target. You'll have the opportunity to discover for yourself the situations that will take you away from your target when they arise."

Louis was beginning to catch a glimpse of the approach advocated by his colleague. And he liked it. There were still a lot of fuzzy elements in his mind, but what Denis had just told him seemed coherent. The idea of being a little dogmatic, uncompromising on the approach, was also exhilarating. He had the impression that thousands of questions were jostling in his head, but he found it difficult to formalize them. And, above all, it wasn't what the project manager had asked him to do.

"Okay, I understand your idea. But what do I tell the project manager? He wants numbers, in dollars. He didn't ask me to bring him the Tables of the Automated Testing Act, with your Dogma!"

"You tell him that what he's asking for is contradictory to the agile approach you want to adopt. Asking for the cost of something before you even define the content, Scrum or Waterfall, is a contradiction in terms anyway. Tell him to go to hell," Denis added loudly.

"I'm not going to say that!"

"What does your boss think about test automation? She's the boss of the initiative, isn't she?"

"She believes in it. She wants us to have an overall DevOps approach. She gave me the assignment to get us into automated testing."

"Then go to her. If you believe in it, tell her what we just said. Tell her your strategy. Tell her about capacity rather than cost. Tell her about target and attitude rather than inventory of tests to automate. Make her your ally. You'll arrange yourself with the project manager later."

"What if she doesn't buy it?"

"Change jobs! Life is too short to waste time doing stupid things, don't you agree?"

Decidedly, Louis found his colleague quite direct in his remarks. He had had few opportunities to rub shoulders with him until now. Denis sure didn't seem to be in the half measure! For Louis, it was both disturbing and exhilarating. As for Denis, he could see from Louis' face that his latest idea scared him a little.

"More seriously," Denis continued, "tell yourself that there's a lot of work to be done in our organization. You see, your project, it's big, it's going to take you several years. So sit down for a few moments and imagine yourself struggling with an approach you don't believe in... Several months, several years... We agree, it doesn't make you want to do it! It's now that you have the opportunity to direct it in an interesting way, at the beginning. So take advantage of it. If you don't succeed, if they don't follow you, at least you've tried."

Louis and Denis parted on these words. Louis was enthusiastic. He felt that he had glimpsed a more consistent approach to the test than what had been proposed to him so far. Above all, he did not like to make cost estimates at the beginning of the project. He found it time-consuming and too uncertain. He always felt that he had to make too many assumptions, and that he was making assumptions that never came to fruition. The capacity approach made his life easier. He still had to convince his boss though. Tomorrow he would go and talk to her.

Denis, for his part, was a bit circumspect: it was the first time he had been so direct with one of his colleagues who had come to him for advice. He wondered what effect it would have. From his point of view, because of the many presentations he had had to attend, it was all taking a bad turn. The consultants were going through their process of selling the automated test, leading to nothing except billing. Denis knew this all too well and he was annoyed. In a way, maybe Louis needed to be shaken up a bit, as did the Company.

TO REMEMBER

· *Dogma and intransigence, even on the surface, make it possible to agree on the target to be reached and the means to achieve it. Half measures are an enemy in the context of transforming practices.*

· *Automated testing is not linked to the software delivery model. The approach to automated testing must adapt to it. It is important to adopt the same values for the practice of automated testing in agile approaches based on capacity, pace, and continuous improvement of delivery practices.*

· *A margin of error is necessary. The number of people on the team should be greater than you envisioned. Indeed, those who fail to become automated test developers will always have a place in the organization. If, on the other hand, you are fortunate enough to successfully convert everyone, your organization will be happy to place your excess developers in its many initiatives requiring qualified personnel.*

· *The important thing is to get started and then look for continuous improvement.*

2

- -

As Louis went downstairs for coffee, he thought back to the two weeks since his conversation with Denis. He had taken the time to think about the information he had received that day and had started by doing what his colleague had suggested: having an open discussion with Jung, his manager.

While he was waiting for his order, he heard someone calling out to him.

"So you haven't given up yet?"

It was Denis. He had just seen Louis and, with a certain malice and a hint of curiosity, he took the opportunity to check up on him. He wondered if he had managed to convince him.

He said, "Hey, Denis, would you like a coffee? Do you have five minutes? I talked to my boss, and she's on board!"

"You see, it wasn't that difficult..."

Louis smiled and they sat down at a table in the cafeteria.

Louis began by reporting his progress over the past two weeks. He had taken the time to explain to his colleagues the testing approach he was going to take and, with Jung, they had supported his approach: all-in! This seemed to them to align with the Company's aims. More importantly, it was more refreshing than the testing strategies with which they were used to being presented.

The idea of taking twice as many testers as seemed necessary had been accepted by the team. It had been harder with Jung, but his explanations were enough to convince her. Indeed, she had understood perfectly well that, as she was not used to automated testing, quantifying the number of testers was difficult and that learning would perhaps leave a few on the side of the road.

"She's a smart boss, and you seem to have made her an ally."

"Yes, and she made it clear that she already knew in which groups to send testers who couldn't make the transition. She has a good overview and knows what others need. Also, when I told her that we could have more people who could do automated testing than we needed, she laughed and said that she knew even more groups that needed it... So I started building the team."

On this subject, Louis had very specific ideas: he wanted above all to find motivated people who were ready to take up the challenge of technical learning. He knew that, to move a project forward while spending time learning Java programming and its environment, he had to be self-sacrificing.

The other important point for Louis was to give the current employees a chance. After all, he had been a test analyst himself, and he was familiar with the routine of manual testing and the desire for change after some time spent in the industry. According to Louis, it was important to demonstrate that it was possible to make the transition to an automated testing practice with employees already in the organization.

Denis listened attentively to his colleague. Louis seemed enthusiastic and Denis liked it.

"You're right, and it will save you a few imposters," commented Denis.

"Impostors?"

"Yes. It's a particularity of fashionable skills. Since everyone is looking for automated test developers, they all claim to "know their stuff". And since recruiters generally don't know any more than you do today, they let themselves be fooled by the first person who comes up with a few generalities found on the Internet."

Louis suspected that Denis was referring to the consulting firm that had made a presentation to them a few weeks earlier. Denis continued:

"Once you're in that situation, since you don't necessarily have the keys to detect it, it could take you a long time before you realize that 'the impostor' doesn't know what he's doing. At least you know what to expect when you take beginners openly."

Louis continued his account of the past two weeks. After several interviews, he finally had the core of a team. He had chosen three new graduates and three experienced testers, all of whom were new to automation. To his small troop, he had added a test data manager, with the objective of facilitating the daily life of the team. Louis felt that what was often a problem in manual testing could not be made easier in automated testing.

"You don't know how true it is," commented Denis, "managing test data is not easy. But we'll have plenty of opportunity to talk about it again soon."

"I think I'm missing someone," continued Louis. "I find myself with several motivated people who want to do automation, but don't really have the skills. And as you know, I'm not going to be able to teach them anything."

"That's not what we're asking you to do. That's not why you're here."

"Yes, but I am the one who has been entrusted with the transformation of this practice in our group."

"Your role, Louis, is to encourage them, to steer the ship. You're the one who's going to animate the group and get them moving. Tell me more about those you have chosen."

"You know, I've mainly focused on checking their motivation and team spirit. These are two important criteria for me. Because I'm pretty sure that it's going to be a long adventure."

"Yes, you did the right thing. I don't want to discourage you, but you'll definitely need the will. What do you think they're missing?"

"They've hardly ever written a line of code. Maybe in university, but you have to admit that in the world of manual testing they didn't have the opportunity to practice a lot."

"So they need to be taught how to code and how to use development tools. What else do you think they lack?"

"The automation side. I guess it's not everything to learn how to code. There must be some specificities for automated testing, right?"

"There are a few. But nothing that great, you know. So they've never seen or done automated testing.

And their programming knowledge, at best, is not very fresh anymore..."

"Do you think I should have recruited people who had already done it?" asked Louis. "Do you think I made a mistake?"

"Right away the big words... What do they need? To learn? Then teach them."

"But I can't teach them Java, I was utterly horrible at programming at the university... A developer could, I couldn't ..."

"A developer, you say?" repeated Denis with a big smile.

"I tell myself that a developer won't want to do testing," Louis objected, "and what's more, I don't see myself asking management for a developer after having asked for so many testers."

Denis was getting annoyed inside. He was well aware that Louis was putting up barriers himself. Why not dare to ask for a developer for his team when he realized it was the right thing to do? He remained understanding, however. Denis had worked for a long time in test groups, and he knew how too often testing was considered an adjustment variable. When it came to saving time or money, the test was unfortunately the first victim. It was always necessary to do it faster, cheaper, and under pressure; proposing an investment was often doomed to fail. Although the context had changed, old habits still remained.

"Look, Louis, I think it's a really good idea to get a developer. There will be a lot of advantages to it. First of all, you're going to be able to rely on someone technical, and the two of you will be able to make better decisions. Second, it will strengthen your team and help your testers learn. It's an exciting challenge to take on, and it can be interesting for many, believe me. He will very quickly grasp how a testing framework works and you're going to need it. Finally, you're going to be able to ask him to liaise with my team."

Louis remained silent for a moment while finishing his coffee.

"You're right, I'll think about it," said Louis.

"Don't think about it. Just do it!"

Denis took a liking for appearing provocative to his colleague. He had noticed that their first meeting had produced its little effect. Louis had acted and seemed to like it. However, their last exchanges had not been well received. Some thought they were fighting. Denis' and Louis' superiors had been informed of this and were concerned about the situation.

"Hey, weren't you supposed to be angry with me," Denis asked. "I found out that I had upset you."

"It's funny you should ask me that, I've heard the same thing about you."

While telling him the whole story, Denis thought it might be time to add someone from his group to help him full time. If Louis could get a developer on his team, then all the odds would be in their favor.

TO REMEMBER

· *Although existing technical skills are assets to initiate a shift towards test automation, the motivation of team members is one of the important keys to success.*

· *Too often, we limit ourselves, out of habit or resignation, to what we believe we can do or ask for.*

· *The commitment of management is essential to the success of a transformation, its support is indispensable when you identify unusual needs. These needs can be human or material.*

· *It is a good idea to build a heterogeneous team, with varied skills and experience. Bringing together people comfortable with testing, others more experienced in development, and finally, referents for test data management is a good example.*

3

"What are you eating for lunch?" asked Louis.

"It's rice, with a sauce the way my country does it: tomatoes, onions, chilli, okra, and, above all, spices."

Almost the entire test team had gathered around a table in the cafeteria. They took advantage of lunch to gradually get to know Mona. She had joined their group at the beginning of the week. Seconded by Denis, her mission was to help them set up test automation.

The team still didn't really know what to expect. They had been working on the project for several weeks. They had attended almost every kick-off meetings. They were starting to get a clear picture of the product and how they were going to test it. They had even started writing the high-level test cases they were planning for the first features.

Mona had been presented earlier this week as an expert in automated testing, but so far she hadn't written a single one. She had spent a few days looking at the tests already written in Jira. Her new colleagues saw her taking notes in a blue notebook. Sometimes Mona would go to any member of the team, looking for explanations of what was written.

"So tell me," Louis asked, "do you think we'll be able to automate the tests we've written?"

"Automating them shouldn't be a problem, I think. From what I understand of the product, the technology won't be a big challenge..."

Louis, like the rest of the team, had noticed a little wavering in Mona's words.

"And apart from the technological side, you're already identifying problems in what we may be doing? "continued Louis.

Mona remained silent for a few moments.

"I've watched almost all of them since Monday. And for manual tests, they are well written. But I'm afraid it won't work for automated tests."

With these few words Mona had just captured everyone's attention. She continued.

"You see, when we do manual tests we try to optimize our actions. For example, we're going to do several checks in one test. And that's often to avoid having to disconnect, reconnect, and redo the whole course before reaching the next checkpoint. That's how your tests are designed. They avoid having to redo the same actions, it saves time when you do manual tests. But for automated tests that's not what you want.

When you do automated tests, one of the big aspects to master is the analysis of results. If you make scripts that check several elements, when there is only one thing that fails in the test, the whole test will be reported as failed. Even if this failure just concerns the color of the validation button of the form for example.

If you do manual tests, it's easy: the tester reports a bug for the button's color and continues his test. The automated test script doesn't do that. It will stop to say that one of its assertions is not verified. That's why every automated test script must have a clear and unique objective."

"Then we're going to have to write tons of tests!" exclaimed Michelle. "It's going to be endless... For example, when we have to check elements of a form, we check a lot of things... A test script for each check..."

Michelle had a strong background in software testing and was known to be very organized, precise, and meticulous. She often had a broad view of products she was testing, without neglecting details. She was highly respected by her colleagues, so her remark cast a chill.

"Not necessarily," Mona calmly continued. "It's a real question what is considered as a test... Let's take the example of the form: you usually want to check three things. First, that the action associated with the form behaves as expected - that's the functional aspect. We will probably have several tests to verify this aspect: with valid data, what you often call the happy-path, but also with alternative or invalid data.

Then, on the form itself, we have a whole bunch of things to check: that fields controls are compliant, that limits imposed on the possible values are properly applied. Many of these checks can be grouped in a single test. So we won't have one test for each checks, but one objective per test, no more."

"Only one test per objective?" Louis worried.

"No, be careful," Mona continued. "Only one objective per test, but the same objective can be found in several tests, because not everything can be verified at once."

"Okay, I understand better: one objective per test but several tests to cover a feature. And you were talking about a third aspect?"

"Yes, in some of your tests I've seen things that suggest checking the appearance of the page or the form, for example. So we're going to do those tests separately as well. It's a different theme, a different objective, so other tests…"

"Can we check the appearance of a web page with an automated test?" asked Steve.

Steve was the technical referent, with software developer experience. He had agreed to join the test automation group with interest when Louis approached him with an offer. His curiosity, both for this discipline that he didn't know and his desire to play a role in training his colleagues, easily convinced him.

"Yes, we have tools for this that use artificial intelligence, but they are very simple to integrate. I'll show you sometime.

But let me come back to the subject of analysis: the ideal would be for tests to be atomic enough, to check something specific enough, so that the name of the test allows us to know what failed when it happens. Because believe me, going through the execution traces to find out what failed takes a lot of time!"

"It's still going to be a lot of scripts to write," Michelle objected. "Won't it take us too much time to write all those test scripts, atomic tests as you say? And besides, won't it take too long to run?"

"I guess we can reuse code, like we do in development," Steve began.

"Yes, absolutely," Mona continued. "We have the Page Object concept for example. It allows you to reuse a lot of code parts that identify elements in a web page. But all mechanisms in libraries make it possible to create reusable pieces too.

As far as execution time is concerned, the practical side of automated scripts is that they can be run in parallel. A bit like hiring as many people as you have tests to do, but for only a few minutes. With manual tests it's impossible, but automated tests allow us to do it. So in fact, we'll most likely get results of our suite of tests faster than if we ran them manually."

With these explanations Michelle seemed reassured. Of course, she had to see and do to be definitively convinced: it was her way of mastering things. But she felt that her new colleague knew the subject well and didn't seem surprised by her questions. Most importantly, she was beginning to see some power in the automated test that would allow her to do things that had seemed impossible previously.

"But tell me," she continued, "can you imagine writing tests that will use different input data? Because then we'll be able to run a test with all the data we can. And that's something you can't do manually."

"You can actually run a test with different input data. We can also give the expected values in each case. This makes it possible to have a single script for several different cases to test. This is called Data Driven Testing. And there are some cases where this is very useful.

But beware! A test must bring something. Adding input data with the only effect of increasing the number of tests performed is useless. Don't fall into the trap of exhaustiveness: as you know, exhaustive testing is impossible. This remains true when you do automated tests."

TO REMEMBER

· *Doing automated tests is not the same as automating manual tests.*

· *Manual tests are often written to optimize manual actions. They take advantage of the exceptional capabilities of the human brain: quickly analyzing complex situations and making decisions.*

· *Automated tests stop at the first error encountered.*

· *It is better to favor tests that are as atomic as possible: one test for one objective, or even several tests per objective if necessary. This makes it easier to analyze results.*

· *Parallelism of execution, the use of Patterns as PageObject, or the creation of reusable libraries are important levers of automated tests.*

4

The invitation had been sent to Louis and Denis with the title "Test Tools", without any other form of precision. A one-hour lunchtime meeting, organized by the project manager, with the comment "Only available slot for this week".

Usually Denis refused this kind of meeting. Firstly, because his days were so busy that he didn't take a lunch break, and secondly, because he knew in advance what he was going to hear. He said it could wait a week or two. But Louis was sympathetic to him; he didn't want to leave him alone with the project manager.

The project manager's role was to organize the initiative's activity: planning, managing the budget with accountants, making sure that he had the human and material resources needed to carry out the initiative. He seemed to take his role to heart: he was at the origin of the consulting firm's intervention. He had insisted that consultants carry out presentations, which Denis and Louis had had to attend, around the automated test.

He had also given a preliminary mandate to this consulting firm, with the objective of producing a study of various existing test automation tools. They were also given a mandate to propose an organization of delivery and test groups for this initiative. It was even suggested that the development and integration of the solution be entrusted to an external service provider, a mandate for which, obviously, the consulting firm seemed well placed.

All of this had been partially put aside when Jung, who was responsible for the initiative, announced that the Company's objective was to be in full control of the delivery of its product. This, by its very nature, ruled out the option of outsourcing everything to an external service provider. Many colleagues had joined Louis to take charge of development and integration.

"Thank you for shifting your lunch hour," the project manager started to say to Louis and Denis. "You were not available at the same time this week outside of this time slot and I wanted us to take decisions without delay."

Denis and Louis, for their part, had the feeling that they would be deprived of lunch, as their schedule was already full for the rest of the day.

"As you know, we had mandated the consulting firm to conduct a study to help us choose the best tool on the market. However, it seems that directions have changed a little and I would like us to be able to justify the investment we made. In particular, I think it is urgent to determine which automated testing tool we will use. I learned Louis that you created your team. Make sure that they have mastered the tool we will select, it's important."

"Yes," replied Louis, "in fact I've taken people who are new to automated testing, they mostly have experience with manual testing but we've set a goal to train them."

The project manager was perplexed; usually in the Company teams were made up of experienced people. However, this was not the first time he had been told of a decision that seemed absurd at first glance.

"Okay, but you know that the consulting firm proposed candidates for your team? They also offered to help us with training for the tool that came out of their study. By the way, have you had a chance to read their report? Were you in the email distribution?"

"Yes," answered Denis. "It's pointless. We can do without it. The firm we hired on these mandates obviously had in mind the idea of selling us other things. Let's quickly summarize what they sent us. To put it simply, they sold us two weeks of work by two of their full-time guys to deliver a PowerPoint document.

In this document, they listed four automated test scripting tools: three paid tools and one free tool. For two of the three paid tools, without looking far, I can tell you that they have no business being there. They're probably just foils."

Having worked with these firms during the early years of his career, Denis was very familiar with their consulting practices.

He explains, "A foil is when someone tries to sell you a less interesting product. A quick search on the sites of the editors of these two tools should make you understand.

As for the last paid tool, they compared it against Selenium, which they considered a free automated test tool. It's a good thing that the test framework my team makes available uses Selenium. But look closely: as if by chance, the paid product appears in their study to be more efficient than Selenium. They want to sell their product..."

"I think you're ascribing them bad intentions, we buy our licenses directly from software editors, without intermediates. They don't have any sale to make here…"

"Make no mistake," resumed an annoyed Denis. "The consulting firm in question is listed as a Platinum Partner of the editor. In cases like this, a prior agreement often exists between the editor and its partners. It stipulates that all they have to do is notify the editor of their pre-sales action to receive a commission on the transaction once it is concluded. And of course, as Platinum Partners, they are entrusted by the editor with training or services related to the software in their geographical area. Haven't you ever noticed that these famous Platinum Partners are generally spread over the territory without really competing with each other? No wonder they told you that they have consultants to help you use the tool."

For his part, Louis had never liked to have consulting firms taking care of almost everything. While he felt some responsibility for the product, he felt he was losing control of it. However, he hadn't considered this aspect that Denis exposed by showing its inner workings.

"But the business case seems solid," insisted the project manager. "The figures show us, regardless of what you say, that the tool they are proposing will bring us a return on investment in automated test writing compared to the free tool, Selenium."

"All right," Denis seemed to agree. "Let's put aside the fact that they're judge and jury. Let's just take their figures: the benefit they estimate largely covers, after a few months, the cost of the license. But they calculate this benefit by taking as a reference the cost of doing the same thing with the free tool. And that's where the problem lies..."

"How? The figures are wrong?" asked Louis.

"No, they're not wrong. They just don't compare the same things. Selenium is not an automated testing tool. It's a library for manipulating Web browsers. You can't compare it to a complete tool. It lacks a lot of features to make it comparable. It's called a test framework."

Denis began to draw an explanatory diagram on the board in the meeting room :

"A complete framework starts with a language. Pretty much any software programing language can be used for automated tests. The right choice is to take a language that is widely used in your team, your group and the Company. Here, we mostly do

Java, but if we were more .Net oriented, you could do the same in .Net.

Then your tests will be written in a particular format. This is literally the test framework. To make it simple, in Java you have mainly the choice between JUnit and TestNG. Both are widespread and known by developers, because they are also used for unit testing.

Your scripts will be part of a development project because to run them, technically, you will compile a Java project. So your testing project will use a tool like Maven. Maven is a software product building tool: your test suite will be a software product like any other.

Your test scripts will then have to manipulate the application to be tested. You will use libraries to do this. Selenium WebDriver is most often used for web applications. That's what they put in their study, explaining that everything else, which I've mentioned, still had to be built. That's why they said that the cost of implementation was higher than with the paid tool... So obviously, they didn't evaluate two comparable things."

"But you'll have to pay for the licenses for all the tools you mentioned," the project manager remarked. "And it seems to me that building this whole framework, as you say, is going to take us some time, whereas the tool they offer…"

"All the tools I mentioned are open-source[1]. And free! As for assembling them, it's already done. I told you earlier that my team provides a complete test framework that includes everything, as well as a data management system, automated reporting... And the whole thing integrates with the other tools of the organization. And then they overlooked important aspects in their study: how their tools fit into what we already use, such as Jenkins, Jira, Git, and most importantly, whether they will be adapted to the technical skills of our employees."

It was on this point that Denis insisted the most. According to him, it was essential to take into consideration the Company's development habits, as well as the employment pool, when choosing a language or a tool. Other criteria, such as the popularity of the tool, which forecasted an active community of users that favoured the availability of exchange forums, for example, followed. There was no magic formula, nor was there anything that could be called "the best tool on the market".

Denis outlined a few personal principles: by nature he did not like products with a paid license. However, he did recognize their usefulness in some very specific cases. He was also wary of "all-in-one" products, which he considered to be generators of

---

[1] Java has open-source implementations. See OpenJDK for example.

captivity. Finally, more than anything else, he avoided what he called "non-portable" solutions, meaning those that only worked on one type of operating system, for example, or when the format produced could only be used in the publisher's tool.

"You see," concludes Denis, "the tool they recommend uses a derivative of Visual Basic. And at the Company we are 95% Java. For that reason alone, their selection is not relevant."

"But then, if I understand correctly, you're suggesting that we ignore their recommendations and burn the investment we made in entrusting them with this mandate," summarized the project manager.

"It's their report that you can burn," Denis replied. "The investment burnt the moment we gave them this mandate. You would have saved time and money by coming to ask us what we had available. But that's okay, it's done. The important thing is not to persist in making mistakes."

TO REMEMBER

· *Choosing the tool is often considered the most important thing. Many people spend too much time and money trying to find the best tool. Finding the right tool, however, is enough.*

· *Salespeople will always tell you that their tools do miracles, that they reduce test writing time, that they do not require training. These promises are only binding on those who believe them.*

· *Open-source tools are capable of covering almost all of your use cases. Most of the time these open-source tools are leaders in their market, far ahead of paid tools.*

· *Considering the job pool and the reality of your organization are essential elements when you will have to make choices: language for scripts, execution framework...*

· *Do not hesitate to question your investments and make the necessary adjustments. Your mistakes will probably cost you more if you are slow to recognize them.*

5

The room that Louis had reserved was large enough to accommodate the ten people who were to participate in the event. It included a large whiteboard and all the necessary equipment to project content from a computer. Louis rearranged the tables in a user-friendly layout. Everything was ready to work effectively as a team.

"Today is the day!" said Louis enthusiastically. "Today we're starting for real. We are going to write our first automated tests!"

He wanted to officially launch the beginning of test automation, and to make an impression on both his team and the delivery group. After all, they'd been talking about it for several weeks. Now they needed to show that it was becoming a reality.

"I remind you of our common goal," continued Louis. "Each of us has to write at least one automated test case by the end of the day. Mona is there to guide us in using the tools and writing the tests. Steve has already identified the features for which we are going to do the first tests."

"I've chosen some features that I think are fairly simple," commented Steve. "I didn't want us to get stuck at the beginning."

"Besides," Mona added, "it's often more meaningful to start with real-world cases. We should make good progress today."

The team seemed motivated, but Louis felt that some of his colleagues were worried that they were not up to the task. Many hadn't written a line of code since university. However, Louis also saw this as an opportunity to encourage peer support: those who could do better should help their colleagues.

Internally, Louis also had some misgivings. By announcing the day to his colleagues in charge of the initiative and posting the objectives, he had created some pressure. He no longer wanted his team to remain an easy target, but rather that the test be at the forefront of the parade. He was still afraid that failure would reflect poorly on his team, his choices, and the automated test in general.

"Here are the rules for today," said Louis. "I've made sure we have this room for the day and not many people know where we are. I want us to be relaxed. I ask you to not answer your e-mails and to work only on what's going on here. If someone is distracting you, by instant messaging or by phone, send them to me. We have plenty of tea and coffee here and some snacks. Finally, it is essential that you have fun throughout the day!"

"I'll start by announcing today's agenda," Mona continued.

Together with Louis, she had worked a lot on the preparation of the event. They had tried to anticipate as many problems as possible. They knew, for example, that within the Company, security rules and procedures could make it difficult to install software. They had made the appropriate requests for all team members several days before the event: installing the software, getting access to the source code manager, the Jenkins server, and a whole bunch of other little things needed for the event. They had had some difficulties; some access were usually reserved for developers, and in the minds of many, testers were not developing code. Here again, Louis realized how far he still had to go in the organization.

Mona had spent some time with Steve, the group's development expert, to familiarize him with automated testing in general and the company's framework in particular. She also prepared the day's agenda. It had to be appealing and have a rhythm. Several theoretical concepts had to be addressed, and she had made sure to almost always include practical cases.

Finally the day began, which was a relief for Louis. Each participant listened attentively to Mona's explanations. For the occasion, he himself had set everything up on his workstation and was ambitious to learn as well to participate. In a way, he was setting an example, and the team had no doubt about the importance of test automation in the future.

From the very first practical sessions, some of them had technical problems, such as a badly configured access or a too old version of a tool. Steve and Mona quickly resolved these problems, since they had expected this kind of incident. There was a studious, informal atmosphere that the team really liked.

Shortly before the break Jung entered the room. As head of the initiative, she managed the 50 or so people in the software delivery group, but she was also responsible for the company's activities with the product, and therefore the associated turnover. Being very involved, she had listened with interest to the automation orientations that had been presented by Louis' team.

"You didn't tell them where we were, did you?" asked Louis.

"No, I did not," said Jung, smiling. "No one but me will come by and bother you today."

The team was a bit surprised to see Jung.

"I know we don't know each other well," she said, looking at the team, "but Louis and I talk regularly. I wanted to tell you that, like you, I am enthusiastic and I wanted to come by to cheer you on."

Shy smiles and thanks emanated from the group.

"Thank you very much Jung. Would you like to spend some time with us and participate?"

"No thanks Louis, I don't want to bother you more than I already have. I see you have some coffee left. Don't hesitate to get more if you run out during the day, it's on me."

With these words Jung let the small group get back to business.

The whole team was focused on doing well. However, after the lunch break, progress was not as evident as desired. For some, getting to grips with the tools was not so obvious, while others did not know enough about the product to make rapid progress. By day's end, half of the team had managed to write at least one automated test. One team member managed to write six. But the other half had encountered a variety of difficulties that took time to resolve. Louis felt it was important to not push too hard. He didn't want to demoralize them and he felt that they were getting tired. He was a little disappointed, as he really thought the goal would be achieved.

Just as Louis was about to announce the end of the day Denis made his appearance.

"I had a hard time finding you," he began. "You were well hidden. It's a good thing Mona texted me to tell me where you were. I went to your floor, the rest of the group is looking for you. Apparently they miss you. Hey, you're making a face," he said to Louis.

"We didn't get it all done," said Louis.

"But you did some anyway, reassure me."

Mona began to detail what they had achieved. In the end, twelve tests were written completely, but by only half the team. The others had encountered various technical difficulties, and some were very close to achieving the goal.

"I had a problem with a conflict with the source code manager," began one of the team members. "I had to do a bad manipulation at first and now I can't get the core project back. I followed up with my colleague who wrote two of them today. But personally I haven't finished one of them."

"Did you understand what was done," asked Denis. "Would you feel able to do it again, under the same conditions, without these problems?"

"Yes, I certainly would. It's just the reason for the conflict that I didn't understand, nor how to fix it. But I think we'll have time to work that out later with Mona."

Mona nodded, confidently.

"For my part," said Michelle, "I finally managed to finish one, but it wasn't easy."

Michelle began to list the various difficulties encountered in configuring the accesses and environment variables to make a Maven project work. She talked about the code conflicts that arose in the early practical phases Mona proposed, and how they had to be resolved. Finally, she explained how she had to explore the execution traces to identify why her test script did not work at first.

While listening to this explanation, Mona and Denis were looking at each other with amusement. According to them, having gone through all this, all the objectives were met. At least the goals that mattered were met, not the ones they had announced to make an impression.

"So if I summarize," Denis continued, "you're telling me that as a team you managed to write two tests per person. Of course, we imagined that each person would do at least one, but considering the group, you did double that. Then you had the opportunity to solve a whole series of difficulties which are common but which it is essential to know how to manage. You have made great progress."

"We also realize that automating tests is not just about writing scripts," Michelle added.

"That's very true," continued Denis. "You're going to realize that you have to organize them and structure them in the right way. Share the work too, get used to working on shared code. All this will come gradually but you have probably discovered more today than Mona and I had hoped for. I think it's been a great success."

Mona nodded her approval. Gradually the faces relaxed and satisfied smiles appeared.

"Tomorrow Steve and I will help those of you who are still having technical difficulties," Mona announced. "They should be easy enough to resolve. Then, what I suggest is that we resume in a few days. Normally, you'll see that we'll write many more scripts in half a day, and that everyone will be able to do it. Because of all the difficulties you've encountered today, once they're solved, we won't talk about them anymore."

These words were encouraging and there was no doubt in anyone's mind that they would succeed. As the day drew to a close, a few team members, including Michelle, decided to stay longer, too eager to finish what they had started.

There was no more coffee, what little tea was left was cold and only a few crumbs remained as a reminder of the morning snacks. Seeing this, Louis began to tidy up the room.

TO REMEMBER

· *Automated testing is more than just writing scripts. It is a development project, with all the activities that this entails: using libraries, managing and collaborating on source code, etc.*

· *The first steps can be difficult, this is normal. Whenever possible, get support from test automation specialists or development regulars. All of them will have something to bring to your team who have so much to discover.*

· *The support of management is important. Displaying it openly promotes confidence in the teams that will face many challenges in their transformation to automated testing.*

· *Creating an "event day" to get started is not essential. However, it does allow you to bring together in the same place and in the same space of time the difficulties you encounter at the beginning. Everyone benefits from the resolution of the different problems, which prevents their recurrence.*

6

The room on the 13th floor had filled up for the sprint review. Louis made a quick count of the number of participants and estimated that there were sixty. In addition to the three initiative squads, there were some of the end users of the product, the project management team, Mona, and finally Jung, who never missed a review.

Michelle and Steve were responsible for presenting the team's work. They weren't used to public speaking and Louis knew that having their boss present would add extra pressure. He had prepared them well: the day before, they had reviewed the points to be presented and put in place a plan B if a technical problem arose. But nothing helped; being in front of the audience worried his two colleagues.

Louis had arranged for the test subject not to come last. He didn't want his team to run out of time for the presentation, nor did he want some participants to leave the meeting without seeing their progress. The review had to be marked by the novelty of automated testing, as the time was approaching.

"Now let's hear from Louis, who will present the progress on test automation," introduced the Scrum Master. "We've heard a lot about it and we're all looking forward to seeing it!"

"I'm not going to be demonstrating the advances," said Louis. "I'm going to leave it up to the persons who actually made the scripts. But before I do that, I wanted to share some figures with you. In the report on the screen, let's first look at the number of stories covered during the sprint. You can see that only forty percent of the delivered features could be tested. This means that we are falling behind in the coverage of features. We are well aware of this. But our goal is to close this gap sprint after sprint. Indeed, we think we will save time on regression testing execution, but also during the end-to-end testing phases. And logically we should have less tests to run manually..."

"You don't seem very sure of yourself, Louis..." intervened Jung.

"These are still only hypotheses. It's the first time we've done something like this. In theory it should work and in practice we're doing everything we can to make it work."

"I understand that. You're new to this approach, so you're not yet able to automate all the tests in a sprint…"

"Yes, that's right! I insist on these figures for the sake of transparency. Michelle and Steve will have the opportunity to talk to you about their issues."

"That's right," began Michelle. "We took five stories because we couldn't take any more. And then we wrote the tests in an Excel file. Then we loaded the file directly into…"

"Wait," interrupted Louis with a smile, "I think everyone is eager to see the scripts. Maybe you can run the test suite directly, and then explain how you got there, what do you think?"

Michelle nodded and Steve, although uncomfortable with the presentation exercises, quickly began running the test scripts. He handled his development environment brilliantly in front of the audience, and the astonishment could be seen on faces. Developers were not used to seeing lines of code presented by testers.

When Steve ran the test project, a volley of information appeared on the big screen. Runtime traces were displayed. The product would open and then close. Actions were performed. Here a transaction was sent, there a check was done. All this harmonized like a dance, a technological ballet, in front of a captivated room. At the same time, mysterious signs were inscribed in a corner of the screen, like a score accompanying the choreography of the windows. Finally, the last window to open was a report that displayed "27 test cases Passed". Steve maximized it to occupy the entire screen.

Steve and Michelle could see that the room was totally captivated.

"So," said Michelle confidently, "here are the 27 test cases we wrote during that sprint. They cover five stories. And they're all at Passed."

"How?" said Jung in amazement. "Did you just run the tests?"

"Yes," replied Michelle.

"The twenty-seven?" continued Jung.

"Yes."

"In two minutes?"

"Well... yes."

Mona and Louis looked at each other with smiles on their lips.

"Usually," Louis continued, "these tests would take us about two and a half hours to perform manually. But as you've just seen, thanks to automation, they were performed in two minutes."

"But hey, it was a long time to do," commented Michelle. "We had to work a lot on the scripts. At first we had doubts. And then we had a lot of problems that prevented us from progressing…"

"Which ones?" Jung inquired.

"During the sprint, we have to analyze and understand the user story. Then we have to write the automated tests, and sometimes manual tests, that we also have to run. Because, you know, we can't automate everything. So in the end we don't have much time to code the tests."

"Do you think the developers can help you write the scripts for the automated tests?" asked Jung.

Michelle knew that the developers would have no problem with automated scripts: they were relatively simple developments after all. But she and her colleagues were beginning to really enjoy this activity, and she wasn't thrilled with the idea of leaving it to the developers and going back to manual testing. She remained silent. Louis flew to her rescue, answering in her name.

"In fact, the business analysts are the ones who could help us. They know the product inside and out and could even take some of the manual testing we still have to do off our hands. That would give us more time to move forward."

On hearing this, some business analysts were not very enthusiastic.

"I think it's perfectly possible," Jung replied. "There are quite a few of them and they're ahead of the game. We'll get organized for that."

The audience nodded silently and the Scrum Master put the subject on the agenda for the next retrospective.

"What other problems did you encounter?" Jung continued.

"IDs on objects," Michelle replied. "That's a problem: many objects don't have IDs."

The audience remained silent. No one seemed to know what Michelle was referring to.

"In a web page," Mona began to explain, "the different elements of the page can have a unique identifier. We prefer to use these identifiers to allow our scripts to interact with web pages. When they're not present we have other options, but they're less robust and more complicated to implement."

"Ideally," continued Steve, "all objects should have unique identifiers. This would help us a lot when writing test scripts."

"That shouldn't be a problem," said the lead developper in charge of the application's Web layer. "We don't always put them in because we don't necessarily need them. If it helps, I think we can make it systematic."

"Then I'll include it as an element to be mentioned in the future retrospective," concluded the Scrum Master. "Anything else?"

"I can't think of anything else at the moment," Michelle replied as she looked at her colleagues in the room.

Steve and Michelle began to unplug the computer used in the presentation to make way for the next speaker. Jung took the floor:

"What you've shown us today is impressive. You know, when I met you three weeks ago and you were just starting out on this project, I had no idea that the results would come so quickly. Really, bravo!" Then turning to the room: "that deserves a round of applause, doesn't it?"

Everyone joined in with Jung and gave them a heartfelt applause.

TO REMEMBER

· Testing is an integral component of a software engineering initiative. Therefore, testing has its place in sprint reviews. This is even more true when introducing automated testing. Everyone will benefit from working together.

· Transparency in difficulties encountered, as well as in results obtained, allows everyone to understand the stakes of a test automation initiative.

· This transparency also helps to generate proposals for help and collaboration.

· Delays must be clearly announced and the reasons for them explained. Transforming a team to adopt a new practice is not simple.

7

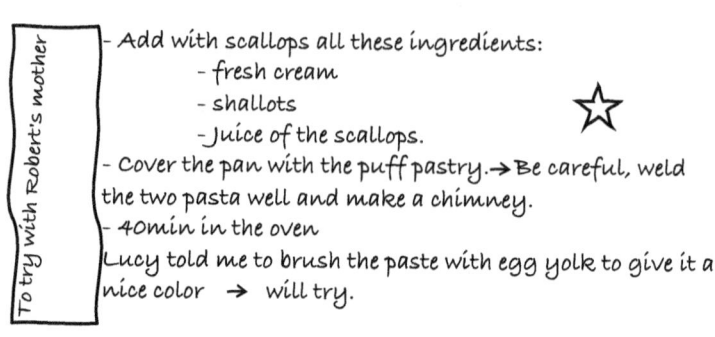

To try with Robert's mother

- Add with scallops all these ingredients:
  - fresh cream
  - shallots
  - Juice of the scallops.
- Cover the pan with the puff pastry. → Be careful, weld the two pasta well and make a chimney.
- 40min in the oven

Lucy told me to brush the paste with egg yolk to give it a nice color → will try.

April 19 - Holidays!

Important - I'm resting this weekend!

Program of the week :

D1 - Proofreading of hackathon's notes. + Review Java course

D2 - Review of tools

D3 - Hiking !! → <u>I won't be able to study</u>

D4 - Practice test cases scripting

D5 - Push the script into the project

To do: google - "test automation university"
Then "Web UI Java Path"

April 22nd - 3:30 pm

Have run hackathon's tests!

Learned loops in JAVA, to share with the team:

- for:

```
for ( start_value; condition; increment_number )
{
  //Action
}
```

- for each

```
foreach (Type variable: arrayOrCollection)
{
  // Action
}
```

- while
```
while ( condition )
{
  // Action...
}
```

- Feed Mousse before leaving
- Binoculars & Compass
  → garage?
- Protein bars
- First Aid Kit
- Trail Map
  → Robert?

70

Questions @ Steve :
1 - What use of break and continue in the loops
2 - Explanation of the labelledLoop

April 23rd
Progress : 4h of videos (15% ~) →Not easy... achievable?
"Introduction to IDE": Mona's explanations++
but this course +++

Seen:
- POM (Page Object Model)
- Locators

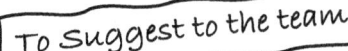
To suggest to the team

Questions @ Mona :
How to retrieve an object from table on the product profile
What is the best way to find a Locator?
ID, Name, Class?

April 24th - **Hiking!**
✓ Feeding Mousse
✓ Phone
✓ Binoculars
✓ Sunglasses
✓ First aid kit
✓ Protein bar
✓ Camel bag
✓ Lighter
✓ Whistle
✓ Headlamp (+ battery!)
✓ Walking stick

Shopping for the weekend:
- 400g of scallops
- carrots
- leek
- white celery
- fresh cream
- shallot
- butter
- Puff pastry x 2
- Milk
- sponge
- laundry
- bread

Tuesday 10am = Dentist
555-2807

April 25th :

Courses I think are not relevant in our case:
- Cucumber
- Robot framework
- Perfusion test

> With that less I should be able to finish before the end of the vacations.

I spent some time on Git → Insist with the team on conflict resolution during commit / push

very useful diagram, <u>to share with the team</u> :

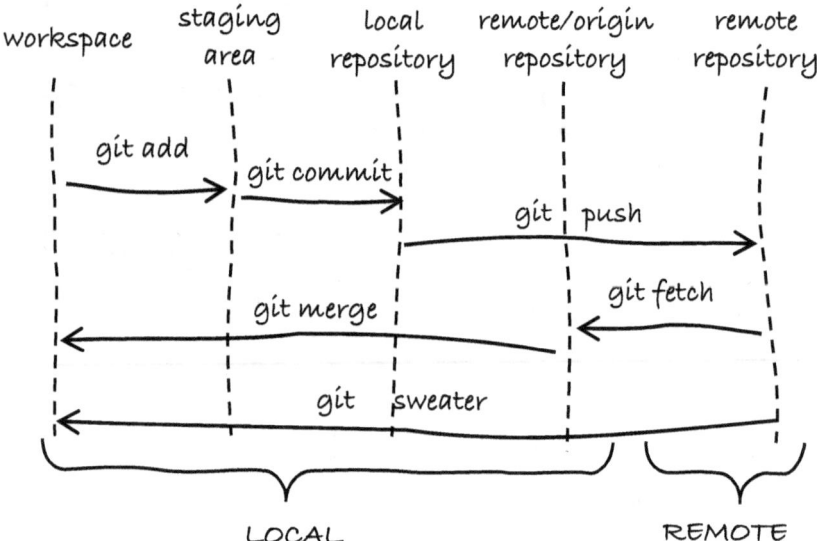

| workspace | staging area | local repository | remote/origin repository | remote repository |

git add → git commit → git push

git merge ← git fetch ←

git sweater ←

LOCAL   REMOTE

April 26th :

Have seen different types of waiters
- wait in seconds (avoid)
- wait on events (better)
API REST
- REST Assured interesting **?**

@ Mona!

Vet appointment for Mousse: FRIDAY
<u>Ask if I need to change his food</u>
White cat specials?
→Beauty contest in 2 **months!**

April 27 - Summary
Web UI Java Path
Done :
- ✓ Foundation
- ✓ IntelliJ
- ✓ Java Programming
- ✓ WebElement locator Strategies
- ✓ TestNG
- ✓ Selenium Webdriver
- ✓ Source Control & Git

Not done:
Visual Testing
Cucumber
Accessibility
Robot Framework
Jenkins
Docker + the rest...

?

Ask @ Mona if relevant...

The Test Automation University site is great. I'll recommend it to my colleagues ++ must see :
- git
- Java programming
- Locators

for Monday:
- Steve's book on JAVA
- Computer
  + Power cable
  + mouse
- Security Badge
- Bring back coffee cup
- Metro Pass

Reminder:
TUESDAY = Dentist!

April 28 - Lucy and her son
Lucy came by yesterday and FINALLY told me why her son left faster on Christmas Eve last year.
I understand better why there was this little malaise!
She told me, a week before the meal, his father had asked him to

73

8

That midday a pad thai faced a chicken sandwich. Louis and Denis had met for lunch break. It had been almost five weeks now since Louis' team had started automating tests. The two colleagues had gotten into the habit of meeting once a week for lunch to discuss their progress and the difficulties they were encountering.

Today Louis had reason to be pleased: he felt that the difficulties of the early days were now behind them. They had now all mastered the use of the source code manager relatively well. In the end, this was the most difficult aspect for his team. In the begining they had accumulated conflict after conflict, no doubt due to a lack of experience. Mona and Steve had been very pedagogical, explaining to each other why conflicts occurred during commit attempts and how to avoid them.

They also had to replace the computer of one of the team members: a software installed during an old project was generating conflicts with the libraries used by the test framework. The IT department had spent several days trying in vain to solve the problem remotely. Steve probably would have solved it faster, but the company's security policy restricted the granting of administrator rights to support technicians located at another site. Annoyed by these endless exchanges, Louis finally decided to order a new "blank" computer to end what he thought was a ridiculous delay.

For the past few days, the writing of the tests had taken on a certain rhythm. Steve had arranged for a task to launch all the automated tests already produced every day at 7:00 am, before the team arrived. Louis was happy to share this progress with Denis:

"You know, I think we're on the right track. We're covering nearly sixty percent of the planned User Stories in each sprint. But I keep asking myself the same question: do you think I should expand the team?"

"Why?" asked Denis between bites.

"Because in the first few weeks our progress has been dazzling. At the very beginning we covered five percent of the User Stories by sprint. Today, because the team has become more competent, we are at sixty percent. But I have the impression that we don't have much room for improvement. So I'm thinking that maybe the team is too small after all..."

Denis had already inspected the week's tests: Mona, whom he had sent to support, regularly reported to him on the project's progress, so he had a fairly accurate idea of what could be holding the team back.

"What would happen if you ran your tests every time you committed code rather than once every morning," Denis continued.

"Ooh, I don't think we can do that," replied Louis. "Every morning, when we get to the office, the tests are usually finished, but it takes us one or two hours to analyze the results and find out what failed. Then we have to write the anomaly reports for development…"

"Two hours a day for writing anomaly reports? You must find a whole bunch of bugs then!" says Denis with a smile.

"No, not that many. Only a few failures are related to product bugs. But we have to sort out those that fail because of a bug and those that fail because of an environmental problem or the dataset. There are still a lot of them and it takes us time."

"Maybe you need to do something about that first?"

"I didn't wait for your suggestion, buddy," answered Louis with a big smile. "I requested that the development team set up a test environment stability project."

"And it's yielding results?"

"Well no, not yet, nobody has the time to take care of it..."

"That's annoying. How about solving your problems first before hoping that others will solve them for you?"

"Go ahead, tell me what we're doing wrong," Louis laughed.

"First off, nightly builds are outdated. What you do by running your tests only once a day are nightly builds. It lacks efficiency. Your target is to run the tests every time you commit code. You can't stop it."

Louis seemed skeptical.

"Before saying that it's not possible, let's look at what's stopping you. Do you think it takes too long to review the results? Let's take a look at what slows you down in that regard.

First your way of naming the test cases. It doesn't make maintenance any easier."

Steve had proposed strict naming rules for test methods. He was inspired by the way packages are named in Java. Each test case had a name that looked like application.module.epic.feature.test That kept things tidy.

"Your test cases have names that are too long, and more importantly, the information is not in the right order. The most significant part of your test case names should be at the beginning, much like a machine name: host.domain.com. By putting it at the end you lose time because test case names are truncated in the reports. You need to open the full reports to find out which test failed."

"I admit that," says Louis. "But do you really think that renaming our test cases will reduce our analysis time?"

"No. Changing your naming rule is going to make your life easier. Anyway, it's useless to rename existing test cases since you're soon going to throw them in the trash"

"Are you serious?" exclaimed Louis. "Is what we've done so far that bad ?"

These conversations with Denis were beginning to amuse him and he was getting caught up in the game, sometimes exaggerating his reactions.

"No," he says. "You did what you had to do to get started: you wrote your first test cases, just as you imagined them. That's important because you set yourself in motion and got through the first technical difficulties. So you learned a lot. But, as you can see for yourself, you're reaching a kind of plateau now.

You're facing your first problems with the maintainability of your tests. Your tests fail too often for the wrong reasons. This is normal because these are your beginnings, but you mustn't let this go on too long. You need to make your tests more predictive, more stable."

"And make the testing environment more stable," Louis asked more seriously, "isn't that a step in the right direction?"

"Yes, but as you can see, it involves several people, several groups that don't have the same priorities as you do. Well... we could debate it, in the end your problems are also theirs, but they don't realize that yet. So they obviously don't have the time, as you say, to work on these issues. On the other hand, you can start to make your tests less sensitive to these environmental hazards. What do you think are the difficulties you encounter most often?"

"Well, often the changes in the web pages make our scripts fail. The development group changes IDs and our scripts fail because of that. We need to identify the source of the failures, then we need to fix our scripts and finally we need to run the tests again ..."

"Start by reducing the number of tests that need web pages. The web pages you use call the application's APIs. When testing features, you should use these APIs directly rather than going through the visualization layer. Any tests you do this way will be insensitive to changes in the pages…"

"But how can we be sure that through the web pages it will work if we check the functionality through the APIs?"

"Testing purpose is not to provide certainty but to reduce risks. When a feature fails, most of the time it comes from the associated API and not from a web page problem. By testing your functionality through the API rather than through the web page you keep a maximum chance of detecting a defect if it exists. You lose a little in coverage, but you recover in simplicity of realization and especially of maintenance. You make your tests more robust to random events."

"So testing via APIs when possible rather than through web pages… Do we need another tool for that?"

"Nope. Our framework allows you to do this kind of test. Rather than using the Selenium library, you'll use the RESTAssured library that we've integrated into the framework. This will allow you to do tests directly on the APIs."

"Indeed," Louis thinks aloud, "I can already imagine the tests we could transform on this model. That's a good part of it…"

"...and you're going to protect them from changes in the web pages," continued Denis, following Louis' lead. "Just like buttons, form field names, or links... These are first actions that will allow you to make your tests more robust and reduce the amount of work for maintenance and analysis of results."

"I'm also thinking about some of the tests we do on asynchronous processing. Today we create the data via scripts that manipulate Web pages, so with Selenium. But then we have to wait for the batch to finish and we check the result directly in the database. We could also use the API to generate the data to be processed rather than the Web pages."

"Exactly! You understand why I was telling you that you probably won't keep the first tests you wrote, and that renaming them wasn't urgent?"

"But we lose what we've done, the investment..."

"No. You've done something much more important: you've learned. You have experimented. You have improved your command of language and technology. You have reached a point where you are learning more about the method. It's well worth the investment. Certainly, if you stayed in this mode, or if you discovered it much later, the price wouldn't be the same. But after only a few weeks of work it's a big step forward."

The two colleagues had finished their meal. There was still some time before both had to return to their desks. Denis continued to give Louis some leads:

"Here's another thing you could do to reduce analysis time: have explicit error messages. The name of the test case isn't always enough to understand what's wrong. Let's take one of your tests."

Denis opened his computer. Louis noticed that his colleague knew exactly where to go to view his team's tests. Right in front of him, Denis unhesitatingly accessed the morning's results and run logs.

"Let's take this one, for example, which failed this morning. Let's put aside the fact that it could use APIs rather than Web pages. We see the 'FAILED' test and we see the error message 'could not find web element <locator>'. An error message like this forces the tester to redo the test manually to understand what is wrong. Not only is this time consuming, but you run the risk that it will work on the second attempt, in which case you would be no further ahead. You may want to try to include more information in the run results. For example: what page the script was on, what action the script wanted to perform, what was the HTML content of the page, or take a screenshot of the page. We've already talked about this with Mona, she will show you how to do this and how to link these elements to the test results. That should speed up the analysis of the results."

"Yes, I guess it will. But let's say the backends fail, won't that generate a lot of execution traces and screenshots?"

"That's also why you might start categorizing your tests. One strategy often used by teams, when the number of tests increases, is to have two or three categories. A first category smoke test, in which you put only tests that will give you an idea of the state of the platform. If you have APIs in five different backends, for example, you're going to take two or three tests that together will "touch" those five backends. If those tests don't pass, it means that one of the backends is down, because it's stopped or something. In such a case your test job should not go any further and should not start the other categories. This prevents you from generating noise and above all it allows you to signal very quickly that the environment has a problem."

"And in the second group I put the real tests, the ones that test the product. Is that it?"

"In the second you put the normal tests, the ones you're going to rewrite. But be careful, make sure you use the stable ones. The ones for which you are certain that when they fail the product has a defect. The ones you made robust. And the third group is for tests that are not very stable or flaky. At the beginning put them all there."

"And move them into the stable group as we go along. That way we can concentrate on flaky tests that fail..."

"No. Focus every morning on stable ones that fail. You need to look at them first and create bug reports. These are the ones that will inform you of a very likely defect, it is this information that you should report first. This is essential! And then the flaky group must be as small as possible."

With these words, Louis left his colleague. He was suddenly less satisfied with the evolution of their work but had several ways to improve the practice of his young team.

Today

Hey, got an idea...

Go ahead. Tell me.

Every two weeks, 2 hours brainstorm with my team, to think about improving what we do.

Great idea. But do it full day.

And don't just think about improving. Do it : spend the day improving your scripts and practices.

Automation Fridays!

 Text Message   Send

TO REMEMBER

· Don't try to have a perfect practice from day one. Give yourself time to learn and gradually see what is best for you.

· Be prepared to revise your ways of doing things, even if it means giving up some things.

· Whenever possible, use APIs rather than GUIs to test functionalities.

· Maintenance is an important activity that will degenerate if your tests are too unstable. Track anything that makes maintenance difficult: poorly designed tests, poor execution logs, unclear test names, unstable data or environments. Act quickly on issues that don't require the involvement of other teams.

· Categorize your tests into three groups: smoke tests (as small as possible), stable, and unstable or flaky. Be careful, stability concerns the test and not the tested functionality. This differentiation allows you to start your analysis with the errors that are most likely to be related to a product defect.

· Work to reduce the number of flaky tests !

9

Standing in front of the board used for the retrospective, Louis put his overly hot tea on the desk.

"Well... several interesting points seem to emerge from our exercise."

The entire test team present in the room nodded. Louis had proposed that they make a retrospective according to the Keep, Improve, Start, Stop model. After two months of activity, it was helpful that everyone took a step back from their operations.

"So if we look at the board and summarize," continued Louis, "for the Keep there is unanimity. You all want Steve to continue R&D and to keep his role of technical support to each of you. I think that makes you happy, Steve!"

"Yes," says Steve, somewhat embarrassed. "I'm glad. I see that I'm helping to speed up scripting. I know I don't participate in analysis sessions with you guys, but it allows me to focus on future issues."

"Well, good for you! So you feel comfortable in this role," Louis said cheerfully.

"In fact," said Steve shyly, "the only thing that's difficult for me sometimes is to justify my time…"

As a coach within the team, Steve suffered the consequences of the organization driven by time sheets: it was difficult for him to justify his activity to project managers. Project managers assumed that time should be allocated to product-related tasks. Scrum Masters were not in the habit of creating team coaching tasks.

He felt really useful within this team: he brought his expertise on development tools, taught a bit of Java, and took care of the more complex technical elements. But since he didn't produce automated tests, and only those were referenced in the product backlog, it seemed to the project manager that Steve wasn't working "on anything".

"We'll make sure your activities are visible in the backlog," Louis tells him. "First, because it will allow us to better manage your time and priorities, but also because it will help our friends in management understand your role and your usefulness in this group. I'll talk to them."

Louis turned to the board and looked at the second group of post-it notes.

"Now for the Improve! You have decided to change the way we validate the results after each build."

"Oh yes," Michelle reacted quickly, "because I'm fed up! It takes an incredible amount of time. I know I'm assigned to this, but I didn't think it would take so long! The last time the new build changed a table in the database, it took me three hours to check everything!"

"So," questioned Louis, "you're proposing that we share the validation, is that right?"

He recalled that the team had tried this approach when they began this results analysis activity. Unfortunately, it had not been very successful. As they took turns doing this task, they found it very difficult to understand their colleagues' scripts. Instead of making it less painful, or accelerating it, it slowed them down and discouraged many of them. At the time, however, they had written only a few hundred test cases. Today they had more than double that.

"Knowing that you had problems at the beginning of this analysis exercise," Mona continued, "what could you do to make it work this time?"

"We could introduce our tests to one another," a team member tried. "If we explain them to each other, it will be easier for us to take turns analyzing the results."

"It's a good idea," encouraged Louis. "What do you think of the idea of taking turns doing the validation? All in favor?"

All hands rose.

"What about the idea of presenting the scripts once a week?"

Once again the proposal was unanimous.

Michelle carefully recorded the decisions made in order to send the debriefing email.

Louis pointed to a post-it in the Start category and addressed the team:

"AN-TI-CI-PA-TION! That's what you wrote. I remind you, we are talking about anticipating the modifications in builds we receive."

Louis hadn't thought about this problem before the team brought it up. He remembered that early in his career, when he was only doing manual testing, he often received deliveries of applications without being informed of made changes. Developers and analysts had agreed on changes, but they didn't take the time to notify the testing team. Louis discovered the changes as he ran his tests and had to adapt accordingly. It only took him a few more minutes. Today, with test automation, it was different. Automated tests didn't adapt to changes on their own and failed, generating hours of analysis and maintenance for the team.

"Now that you've told me, I understand the effect that has on your work," Louis commented. "So, does anyone have any ideas on what we could do to avoid these kinds of surprises?"

A short silence fell. Obviously the team felt that something could be done to stop suffering from changes, but what?

"For example, couldn't we get in touch with the developers to help us?"

"I think it's possible," Steve said. "Developers know what's going to be changed. If we ask them to give us a presentation of the changes, at mid sprint for example, we could anticipate the maintenance to be done."

"That's a great idea! Who's with Steve?" Louis asked, raising his hand.

They all did the same. Louis' enthusiasm was infectious and the team kept up with the decisions with good humor.

Approaching the last group of post-it notes, Louis announced:

"Finally, the famous Stop... You proposed to stop the manual tests…"

It was a hot subject. Louis was in agreement with this idea while remaining cautious. While the team needed to devote full time to automating the tests if they wanted to make progress, manual tests still had to be done.

"The business analysts are already helping us with the manual tests. Maybe they could do them all," suggested one of the team members.

The business analysts had indeed become closer to them and were now involved in the execution of manual tests. At the beginning, it had not been easy: some thought it would be repetitive. But as time went on, most were having fun discovering and reporting defects. In addition, it gave them a better understanding of the product they were designing: ideas came to them for improving ergonomics or simplifying workflows.

Louis promised the team that he would use persuasion to get the proposal accepted. Although some were skeptical, Louis remained confident: Jung had already given them her support and there was no reason for it to stop.

"Before I conclude this retrospective," Louis continued, "I would like to propose an idea. Every week, let's have a day devoted to improving our practices. There are scripts to be optimized, we can improve our programming... this day would be devoted to that."

"But," Michelle replied, "there is no day where we are all free!"

The weeks were indeed busy: Monday and Tuesday, there were working sessions with business analysts. On Wednesdays, a third of the team was not working. Thursday was for planning. And every third Friday, agile ceremonies took up a good part of the day.

"Two out of three Fridays we're all available, I think," says Louis. "Let's keep these days free of meetings. I'll make sure the other groups don't disturb you on those days. We'll only work on improving our practices."

An appointment was made for the following Friday. The retrospective was over. Everyone returned to their workstations.

Finding himself alone in front of the board, Louis began to take off the post-it notes one by one. On the table, his untouched tea was now cold.

TO REMEMBER

· Materialize support and training actions as elements of the backlog.

· Pay attention to the segmentation of responsibilities within your team. This can create bottlenecks and also generate weariness for some.

· The test team will always benefit from collaborating upstream with the development team. This is even more true in the context of test automation.

· Allow time for individual and collective improvement. Trainings, conferences, and team workshops are great communication tools to progress.

Test Automation
Award

This award recognizes the commitment and exemplary attitude of

Michelle

in test automation activities
within the Company.

*"Michelle has shown a keen interest in test automation. Curious and
willing, she has taken advantage of self-training opportunities to increase
her technical knowledge. This is an exemplary behaviour that makes her
a key player in the success of our initiative. »*

10

"Thanks again on behalf of Michelle," says Louis. "It's a great show of appreciation for her efforts. I didn't know you gave out this kind of award, do you give out awards like this often?"

"No, this is only the second time in three years."

Comfortably seated in Chesterfield chairs, Louis and Denis enjoyed a sunny terrace table. They had met after work in a downtown bar.

Earlier in the afternoon Denis, accompanied by a few members of his team, had come to present Michelle with an award. The Automation of Tests Award. This award recognized her commitment. She had decided, on her own, to take some of her free time to train and perfect her skills in the technologies that are useful to her today.

"You're going to put the photos you took on the Company's network again, aren't you?" asked Louis.

He already knew the answer and feared that his team would feel additional pressure. He felt that expectations increased when Denis used them as an example. However, he understood that Denis was using their progress to show the other groups in the company how to proceed. In any case, he knew that if he protested, Denis would take great pleasure in adding to it. As a sole answer, Denis was content with a slight smile.

The waitress set an Old Fashioned and a Maï Taï on the table. In her wake, jazz notes resounded from the room now abandoned by customers. The calm of the terrace was relaxing, and conducive to friendly discussions.

"And how do you get those prices?" asked Louis.

"We made them ourselves, it does not cost much, but you know it's the message that's important. And then, as you saw, Michelle was happy and your team was proud of her. It's important to celebrate this kind of success. It's too often forgotten."

The waitress came back with Iberian ham and black olive tapenade. The discussion was going well: Company projects, family trips, music and outings to do. The glasses had been emptied and Denis signaled for the second order. As time progressed, Louis tackled a more professional subject:

"Do you know when Mona wants to take her vacation this summer? Because I thought that she could accompany the trainee's arrival in three weeks?"

"It would be better if you didn't count on her too much," Denis interrupted him. "I was thinking of taking her out of your group in two weeks."

"What? What are you talking about? In two weeks?"

"Yes, in two weeks."

"But wait... Two weeks is a short time for me to replace her, I'll never find someone so quickly," exclaimed Louis.

"You should rather take it as good news," said Denis amused while helping himself to a piece of ham. "It just means you don't need her anymore. Haven't you realized that she's been around a lot less lately?"

"Yes, a little. But I was thinking that she was working for us remotely."

"She still works for you," confirmed Denis. "But we've agreed with Mona that she's gradually withdrawing. For the past three weeks she's been letting your testers take over the management of the framework. They're doing very well, by the way. She's monitoring their progress. The last report she gave me concluded that you were ready to fly on your own. You know, we don't do anything without purpose."

In fact, for the past few weeks, Mona had been careful not to use her workstation to solve problems in the scripts. She was doing it in front of her colleagues on their own workstations. Additionally, she had made sure that she had almost stopped touching a keyboard, and instead gave oral instructions to the testers. Then, in order to highlight the independence acquired by her colleagues, she made a point of no longer sitting next to them. By remaining standing, the exchange was naturally faster and the feeling of independence grew. Finally, Mona tried to be less and less visible by moving to another location in the open space.

Louis remained silent for a few moments. He had noticed that the velocity of the testers had remained at its normal level. No one on the team had expressed any concerns to him.

"It had to happen," said Louis, "but I didn't expect it to happen so quickly. And I guess you need Mona to assist other groups. Could you help me identify a candidate? Because finding someone like Mona is not going to be easy..."

"I don't think you understood what I just said."

The waitress interrupted them for a few moments to drop off a Cuba Libre and a White Russian. Denis resumed:

"You don't need a coach like Mona anymore. You have acquired the right reflexes, you mastered the framework and you know, other challenges await you."

"You think we don't need help anymore?"

"I didn't say that," Denis amused himself. "You needed a coach because you had everything to learn. Mona was able to bring you that: how to do atomic testing, how to use the development environment, how to handle the source code manager, how to collaborate on shared code... all these things are necessary when you start from scratch. Challenges that await you are about optimizing your practice and better integrating into the software development lifecycle. This is a long-term job that requires the role of a leader rather than a coach. You will have to adjust your strategy, set new standards on scripts, measure the team's efficiency, and increase your collaboration with the development group."

"And a leader is easier to find than a profile like Mona?"

"Not really. But I've got my network, so we'll see if anyone's available."

With these words, as it was getting late, Louis called the waitress one last time and asked for the bill. He insisted on paying for Denis.

TO REMEMBER

· *It is important to value employees who demonstrate personal commitment. Never neglect this point.*

· *You have to accept to grow: there will come a time when your coach will have to gradually withdraw. This will encourage the team's sense of autonomy. However, be careful to keep your coach accessible when needed.*

· *As you begin to become independent, be aware that other challenges await you.*

· *Old Fashioned[1]: Bourbon, Sugar, Angostura, Water. Replace Bourbon with Rye, as Bourbon is for hillbillies.*

· *Mai Taï[2]: Amber Rum, White Rum, Orange Curaçao, Barley Syrup, Lime, Cane Sugar. Always better with Cuban Rum.*

· *Cuba Libre[3]: Cuban Rum, Cola, Lime.*

· *White Russian[4]: Vodka, Coffee Liqueur, Fresh Cream.*

---

[1] https://iba-world.com/iba-official-cocktails/old-fashioned/

[2] https://iba-world.com/cocktails/mai-tai/

[3] https://iba-world.com/cocktails/cuba-libre/

[4] https://iba-world.com/cocktails/black-russian/

11

At the end of each sprint, the whole team would meet for two hours for the initiative review. The room was large but always ended up looking cramped. The project manager, the developers and analysts, and the test team of course, but also the sponsors and the product owner were present, as well as several people involved with the initiative. Once again, unfortunately, this meeting interfered with the lunch hour.

Louis had planned to make an inventory of test automation, since he and his team regularly presented it. Good progress had been made recently, and the team had reached a certain maturity.

While Michelle was speaking, Denis was observing from the back of the room. From time to time, he liked to assist initiatives' reviews that his group accompanied. He didn't always give advance notice, and he arranged himself to know the times and places and tried to be present when his agenda permitted.

The demonstration by Louis and his team came to an end. The time came for questions from the audience. Denis raised his hand. He hadn't come quite by chance. Louis, discovering the presence of his colleague, gave him the floor:
"It's not really a question, more a remark."
Louis did not know what to expect.
"You know, when you run your user interface tests with Selenium, you use our hub. This Selenium hub, pretty much every test team in the organization uses it. Since we're the administrators, we can give you some figures that Louis doesn't know.

Over the last thirty days, fifty percent of the tests executed on the hub came from your scripts. There are nearly twenty active projects, some of which have been running for two years. You alone represent more than half of the activity. All of the organization's initiatives combined do fewer test executions than you do.

I think this is worth noting, and I think we can really congratulate Louis and his team."
Applause rang out, smiles appeared, especially from Jung who was pleased to see the team's progress. Louis was about to take the floor again to

say thanks, but Denis did not give him the time to do so:

"It's all well and good to do automated tests," he continued, looking at Louis with a big smile, "but I'd like to suggest a quick exercise. You know, many people think that automated testing saves money. I'm going to show you the opposite with a little calculation. This morning I took the number of test runs performed by your team. A manual tester, when testing an application, performs between two and ten tests per hour. It depends on the context of course. Let's take a generous estimate of ten tests. Roughly speaking, to achieve the number of test runs you have, it would take fifty full-time testers. That's the equivalent of this room full of testers. Here's what your small group is doing for the initiative."

In the room the audience was conquered. Jung intervened:

"So why do you say that we don't save money by doing automated testing? I see that we save the cost of more than forty testers!"

"Jung, no one would accept having a team of fifty testers for an initiative like yours! In a project where testing would be done manually you would probably have a testing team of the same size. In the end this team would probably do a lot less testing. So you haven't saved money, you've increased your coverage and most importantly you've increased the speed at which feedback is passed on to the development group."

"That's right," nodded the product owner. "In my previous initiatives, developers did not have the test results until several weeks after their commitments. Now you send them to us the next day or two at the latest."

"Let's face it," continued Denis, "this coverage and speed is worth far more than the cost of many testers. The value you get from this group today," he said, pointing to Louis' team, "is to get our product to market faster and give the Company the ability to do business with the solution you design faster. It is because of this, more than the number of tests, that Louis' team deserves our congratulations."

The convinced audience responded with further applause. The part dedicated to the test was over. The review resumed its course covering the subjects in the program.

With a bit of difficulty, Louis managed to join Denis at the back of the room.

"Thank you, it's cool what you just said," he whispered to Denis. "And I'm glad you shared those numbers."

"We have to talk about it," replied Denis with a big smile, "because you're making a big mess, and it's not going well at all."

Louis did not understand, and he couldn't tell if his colleague was joking or not. Denis, on the other hand, had noticed his impatience and pretended to be interested in the rest of the review so that he didn't have to express himself immediately. When there was a change of presenter or a brouhahaha for a few seconds, Denis would rush out to grab a bite of his sandwich. With a few friendly nudges, Louis showed Denis that he was not fooled.

When the review was over, the two colleagues found a quiet place to finish their meal.

"So, what's wrong again?" Louis asked.

"You're running so many tests that our Selenium hub resources are saturated. A lot of tests are failing because there's not enough room for everyone. It's not your tests that are failing, it's those of other initiatives. When you run your tests you use all our resources and you fill the queue. It's just big enough for the number of tests you have. Tests from other initiatives don't find a place in the queue."

"So I understand, we test too well," Louis replied reassuredly.

"In fact, you test too much! And you probably feel it a little: you have to spend a lot of time looking at the results. I think it comes from your change in the execution policy. Remember when I told you that a nightly build was not the best approach in the world?"

"Yes, in fact we quickly changed that, as you suggested."

Denis had indeed seen the changes following his recommendations. Overnight, the number of tests performed had tripled. Perhaps he misunderstood: Louis' team had activated a mechanism that executed the entire test suite every time one of the testers modified it. So that generated a lot of executions.

"But," Louis asked, "isn't that what we wanted to do?"

"Well, yes and no. We encourage you to do Continuous Testing. But it's a little different. The idea is to trigger testing when there's a change in the code of the application you're testing. And not when you change your test scripts..."

"But, isn't it equivalent to triggering execution every time we change things in the scripts?"

"No, for the group of testers it allows them to check that the scripts still work. Situations where your changes affect other tests are quite rare. The

Page Objects are concerned, as well as the utility libraries. Most of the time you add or modify tests that are independent of one another. We have taken care of this very early on.

Continuous Testing aims to reduce the feedback time after a change in the product as much as possible. It is there to serve the development, not the test. It's therefore a question of replaying the tests each time the source code of the application changes. Today you use the Git Flow[1] model in your initiative, both in the development of the application and in your automated test management. You have set up a trigger for your tests each time changes are made to your scripts. By doing this, you have information about your test suite and not about the product you are testing. You know if, after your change, your tests behave in the same way. Is this information really relevant to you? I invite you to think about it with your team."

"I'll talk about it at our next meeting," says Louis.

"Indeed, talk about it, you might find it interesting. You should know that the real information that developers are interested in is not this one. Your developers need to know if their changes in code affect the product, whether it's positive when they fix a defect, or negative when they introduce a regression. The appropriate time to provide them

[1] https://nvie.com/posts/a-successful-git-branching-model/

with this information is as soon as possible after they introduce their change. So your orchestrator needs to observe what is happening in the application code repository and not in the test script repository. It is when they make a change in the application code that the feedback is most relevant to them."

"Wouldn't it be better to give them direct access to test results? That would also be in line with rapid feedback..."

"You are putting your finger here on something very important. That would be excellent. But that's where the difficulty of Continuous Testing lies. What is difficult is to give reliable information. Let's take a quick look at the approaches you've taken so far: you'll understand that they serve exactly that purpose.

First of all, let's make the tests simple and easy to understand. This involves atomic tests, naming rules for your tests, and also error management. All this is essential if you want to do Continuous Testing. As you can guess, the developer has to be able to understand what doesn't work when his change will make one of your tests fail. If he has to wait for you to analyze it for him, it won't work.

Then group the test runs together. It is likely that the tests you want to run on each change are the ones you put in the smoke tests and stable groups.

You don't want the developer to lose confidence in the tests that are triggered at each change because they would be unstable, do you? That's why you should only present them with the results of the smoke test and stable groups."

"So then, we don't run flaky tests anymore? If only the smoke tests and the stable ones are used anymore…"

"Remember, we agreed that the tests you classify in flaky should be as few as possible. That's good, because you won't present all the results of this group directly to the developers. You'll have to systematically review them beforehand. A kind of results certification…"

"I see the idea," replied Louis. "It's extra work, so we'll definitely want to keep this group as small as possible!"

"That's right! But nothing prevents you from allowing any developer to run all the tests, on demand, on any branch. This would allow them to evaluate the branch feature they are working on. But ideally this means allowing the creation of an on-demand test environment, which contains the code of a specific branch."

"It seems complicated to me," replies Louis, a little overwhelmed.

"It's not. Well, not much," answered Denis. "We'll talk about it again. You should be able to integrate that in a little while. But it's probably still a little too early. You should first look at the executions triggered by the changes in the develop branch. That's a great first step. And then it wouldn't hurt to talk to the development group about the branch model you're using. Between us, Git Flow is not the easiest to integrate in a Continuous Delivery logic. And Continuous Testing is a component of Continuous Delivery. You should suggest them Trunk Based Development[1], it's more adequate and it will force them to be more rigorous and much more reactive."

"Do you want me to talk to the developers about the Branching Model? I don't know anything about it !

"Don't worry, we'll go together," answered Denis with a smile.

"You make me do crazy things every time I see you!"

"Let's rather say that if I'm not there you'll do crazy things," Denis laughed.

---

[1] https://trunkbaseddevelopment.com/

TO REMEMBER

· *Continuous Testing consists of performing automated tests from the delivery pipeline. This pipeline is triggered each time the application code is modified.*

· *The primary objective of Continuous Testing is to provide immediate feedback on the code that has just been produced. The speed at which test results are obtained is essential.*

· *The reliability of the results is a key component of Continuous Testing. If the information is unreliable - because of flaky tests for example - then confidence in automated testing will gradually disappear.*

· *The results of flaky tests must be reviewed before they are made available to developers.*

· *Writing automated tests is similar to developing a product. The associated practices are therefore similar, especially the way in which the source code is managed. It is important to adopt a branching model adapted to your needs, and as much as possible, aligned with the one practiced by the development group.*

12

Denis had worked his network to find Mona's replacement. The few people in the Company who matched the needs of Louis' team were already busy. There was no question of putting one group in difficulty for the benefit of another.

The first candidate had been recommended to them by a vague acquaintance of Mona. During the interview, Denis, who accompanied Louis in his recruitment process, quickly detected his lack of practice. He certainly had an impeccable discourse on Continuous Testing and automated testing, yet Denis sensed that something was wrong. As the conversation progressed, Denis made such an absurd statement that Louis raised his head questioningly. The candidate did not seem to be shocked.

"He is one of those 'impostors'," Denis explained during the debriefing with Louis. "I had already told you about it when you first started. People who claim to have implemented these practices but who only read books, without living the adventure that is yours today. You've just seen an example of this. He's not the one you need."

Good candidates were rare. For a long time the testing activities had been considered of little value, so the resources devoted to them were low. Motivated people with little technical knowledge were referred, and others were referred by default. In some companies, Denis had even seen successful testers encouraged to change direction. Only in innovative companies could you find people whose passion and competence in this field were recognized.

Max came from one such company.

"I started in a consulting firm right after I graduated. In the beginning I was a developer, tester, and also a system administrator. I quickly changed companies because I realized that the testing business was the one where I flourished the most."

"What was the reason?" asked Louis.

"Because in this job we're asked to 'break things' and we get paid for it," Max replied with a laugh.

Louis appreciated his relaxed attitude. He differed from the other candidates they had met in the afternoon. This last interview of the day was conducted by videoconference. Max's cat was constantly in front of the camera.

"Please excuse Fantomette," Max continued, "she always wants to be the center of attention. In all seriousness, I get real intellectual satisfaction from tracking down possible problems in a software program. It's much more stimulating than solving them with code."

"And then, by doing automated tests, there are still code challenges to be met," Denis added.

"That's right," Max continued. "May I ask what approaches you have taken so far?"

Max asked a lot of questions and seemed interested, Louis thought. Louis told the story of his group with enthusiasm: the constitution of the team, the first steps, the current situation. When it came to the tools used, Max didn't linger, just nodded. Here again Louis noticed a difference with the other candidates: one of them, for example, had questioned at length the reasons for their choices and put forward a tool using another language that he found more effective.

"What are your current difficulties? "asked Max. He was trying to understand, taking a lot of notes. Denis explained the objectives to be achieved and the elements that needed to be addressed now. The team had made a lot of progress, but the monitoring of its maturity was not in place. Louis felt that they were becoming more efficient, but he was not sure how to measure it. So the two colleagues told Max what they thought were the challenges ahead. Louis ventured:

"Also, I think it might be good for us to run some automated tests in production."

Denis, surprised by this idea that Louis had never before expressed, waited for Max's answer. The latter asked:

"Why do you want to test in production?"

"Well, because sometimes we encounter problems during deployment. And by testing, we detect them and solve them before the service opens."

"What kind of problems? Do you have any examples?"

Louis explained from memory the two problems encountered in recent deployments. One concerned the reconstruction of a database: the scripts had not applied the correct access rights to the service account used by the application. The tests had detected them because the list of transactions was no longer visible. The second problem concerned a backend system that had not rebooted as it should have. Again, manual tests in production had discovered this.

"That's why," concludes Louis, "I imagined creating a production test suite - to allow us to deploy more quickly."

"I don't think that's a good idea," Max began.

Louis looked at him, interested. Denis remained silent.

"You see, there are two reasons why the product might not work when deployed. The first is often the inability of the delivery team to create the right conditions for testing. In these cases, teams are tempted to test in production because 'it's easier'. However, rather than doing that, it is obviously better to work on improving the testing process upstream. That is to say the representativeness of the test environment, the relevance of test data and its accessibility.

The second reason, in my opinion," Max continued, "concerns environmental issues. All the problems you mentioned are part of this. I don't think it's up to the automated tests to detect them, but rather to the monitoring elements built into the application."

Louis wanted to know more, so Max continued. As part of the application, a health-check procedure had to be built. This procedure checked the connectivity of all the elements necessary for the application to work properly and could be called up by a monitoring tool. Databases, WebServices, connections to file servers, everything had to be checked simply by calling this procedure.

"There are several advantages to doing this," Max concluded. "First of all, by being an integral part of the application and its functionalities, there is less risk that maintenance will be forgotten. Second, it will also benefit your test environment. And last but not least, it does not involve an external element to the application, such as your tests."

The interview ended there. After thanking Max, Louis and Denis reviewed the day's events.

"I need Max," said Louis. "It's obvious to me that he's the best."

"He sees beyond testing, that's a good thing. I wouldn't have said anything different for his answer regarding testing in production. And then he has another indispensable quality."

"Which one?"

"He knows how to tell you when you have bad ideas! That will be very useful to us," joked Denis.

TO REMEMBER

· *The recruitment market is sometimes complicated. Pay attention to the people you want to recruit.*

· *People with diverse backgrounds often have the quality of adopting several points of view and not limiting themselves to their current role.*

· *Before you embark on automated production testing, make sure you understand your reasons for doing so. Often you may be able to cover the risks differently. Software quality is not just about testing.*

13

"We need to find a way to stabilize environments," Max seemed to conclude. Denis had heard this phrase as he approached the small group of Louis, Steve, Max and the initiative's development manager. They were all standing around a high table trying to solve the stability issues of the tests.

"So, test environments giving you a hard time?" Denis said as he approached them. "That's something unusual," he continued ironically.

"Ha, you're just in time," exclaimed Louis. "You might be able to help us."

"We've been working on stabilizing our automated tests," explained Steve, "with the goal of doing Continuous Testing."

"Some of the tests have been improved and are much more stable now," Max continued. "But a large part of our tests are still unstable. By doing a detailed analysis we realized that most of the failures and instabilities come from the test data and applications in our test environment."

"Is it the application you are testing that is unstable?" asked Denis.

"No," answered Steve, "it's more the component behind it, the ones we communicate with. But they are not our responsibility. Just look."

Steve presented Denis with the details of their investigations, as well as a schematic of their product architecture. He was communicating with several subsystems already present in the Company or under construction. Three of them seemed problematic.

The first contained data that was constantly changing. Indeed, the team in charge of developing this product had to perform regular data loading tests. This generally resulted in de-synchronization with the data used by Louis' team and consequently led to test failures.

The second subsystem suffered from instability in the test environments. The servers were regularly unreachable, and the team in charge of this application had little time to devote to their maintenance. They tested themselves on other, more stable servers and only maintained the other environments out of obligation.

The third subsystem was not managed by the Company. It was a third-party system for which only one test environment existed. Although it was stable, the availability range did not match the team's needs: the system was shut down outside normal business hours.

"The problem is that they're four time zones behind us," said Louis. "So, office hours yes, but it doesn't match ours. And there's no way we're going to renegotiate this contractual aspect with them; we have no leverage to change that today."

"Over eighty percent of automated test failures come from these three subsystems," added Steve. "A significant portion of the testing errors would be eliminated if we could make the applications more stable and available."

"In short," Denis summarized, "you want to ask one group to stop its data loading activities, the other to spend time repairing and stabilizing a test environment that they are not interested in, and a partner, with whom we have a contractual relationship, to provide us services without any financial compensation. It definitely seems compromised."

"We could consider systematically creating test data before running our scripts," proposed Steve. "That would probably allow us to get through untimely reloads."

"Yes, but the other two subsystems will continue to be unstable or unavailable at certain times. That won't change the problem," replied the lead developer.

The four colleagues seemed quite frustrated. Everyone was silently looking at the numbers and diagrams on the table.

"Why are you smiling at me," Louis asked Denis. " Do you have a solution?"

"You should know what you have to do. We've been talking about it recently," Denis said, laughing.

Louis searched in his memory. Nothing!

"You should consider isolation and replace the subsystems that your application calls for with stubs or mocks. These are small software components that will simulate the response that the subsystem would make. Your application will work as if the subsystem is there."

Denis continued his explanation by taking as an example the architecture diagram presented on the table. He traced on it what he called "borders and boundaries". Anything beyond these boundaries was out of the team's control, so it had to be replaced by mocks. Each of these mocks had to replace a service and respond according to what the actual subsystem would do.

"Isn't there a risk of redeveloping the external subsystem?" Louis asked.

"In fact, Denis explained, except in special cases, recording the system's response in json or xml will suffice. We will then have to load this response into the mocks server, so that it simulates the response to each call. However, some elements will have to respond to a logic that is easy to integrate, such as a date that must be adjusted for each call, or an answer identifier that must be generated each time. Nothing too fancy! And then, as far as security is concerned, you can configure your mocks server to accept all authentication tokens without checking anything."

"And how do you go about recording the responses of all the data that's going to exist," asked the lead developer. "Do we make a script that will make all the calls and keep the answers? It's going to be too big."

"I think we can limit ourselves to the data we're already using," said Steve. "Today we're using about fifty different test data, not much more. Since that's enough to cover the different cases, I guess we can limit ourselves to that?"

Denis agreed. He explained how to go about it: first of all, start by setting up the recorder, a sort of proxy that is placed between the product under test and the subsystems. Using the application, the recorder would capture the call and then the service response. By playing the entire suite of automated tests, the different calls would be recorded. A clean-up work would have to follow, in particular to make some elements such as timestamps or unique response identifiers variable.

"It's true, it's a bit of work, but it doesn't seem insurmountable," says Steve.

"But how do you decide when to replace the subsystems with these mocks," the lead developer asked. "Because we too have to guarantee the availability of our application in the test environment. If we put in these mocks, our application will be isolated and other teams will complain."

"How are you deploying your product today? Do you have scripts for that?"

"Yes, of course, we put this in place very early on to avoid handling errors."

"So, I imagine that you would be able to recreate servers in the cloud, for example, and deploy the product on blank servers?"

"That's already what we do when we deliver to production: we recreate virgin servers in which we deploy the new version. It would be a matter of doing that for a test environment, just for automated testing if I understand what you mean?"

Denis was pleased to see the lead developer buy in and understand the role he had to play. Indeed, he was too often confronted with groups that considered the test as a separate activity, and the collaboration between developers and testers suffered as a result. In fact, introducing Continuous Testing meant that there were several specialists whose collaboration could prove difficult. The exercise could then turn into negotiation sessions between people who never had time for anything. The situation seemed more favorable here. Denis continued.

"You could even go a little further."

He resumed the architecture diagram on the table.

"You see, we've drawn the boundaries of what's under your control. Anything beyond that, we replace with mocks. But if you look at your application, it also has internal boundaries. For example, look at the presentation layer that allows display in a Web browser. This is based on internal APIs. You might very well consider replacing them with mocks. This would allow the group that handles the web interface to test the appearance of the application long before you have finished developing the services underneath it."

"It's easy for me," said the lead developer. "These pieces are clearly independent components. They run in containers. It will be easy for us to deploy them on demand and to connect them to the mocks servers you're talking about."

"...and make this mechanism available to developers," Max continued, "or the product owner, so they can quickly test and comment on the appearance of the product...."

"Easy!"

"Ah, I remember," exclaimed Louis! "That's what we talked about the other day!"

"Well, it took you long enough," said Denis, laughing.

Denis ended the discussion by explaining the few changes that would occur in Louis' team's automated tests. They already had the right characteristics: they were independent of each other, small enough, and always targeted a specific element. It was in the verification phase that the changes would take place. For example, rather than checking whether a transaction had been accepted by the external system, it was now necessary to verify that the message sent by the application was compliant. This was easy to do, as the mocks server allowed the call details to be consulted via APIs. The key to the verification was the interface contract that existed between the two systems. By verifying that the message sent was compliant with the interface contract, the test provided sufficient guarantee that the product was compliant. Of course, it would probably be necessary to maintain end-to-end tests to verify that the systems were communicating correctly, but the vast majority of tests could now be done in dynamic, isolated environments.

"The good news," concludes Denis, "is that you will even be able to test cases that are very complicated to produce. There are actually cases that exist in reality but for which you don't have the data in the test environments. In this case, all you have to do is modify one of the mock records to simulate this situation."

"For once you were just passing by chance," joked Louis, "and you found a way to be useful anyway?"

"Let's just say that it wasn't entirely by chance…"

"Come on, how could you know that we needed help?"

"An intuition," Denis answered teasingly. "An intuition."

TO REMEMBER

· *The isolation of the tests consists in replacing the external systems by stubs or mocks. These elements constitute Tests Doubles[1] that are essential for automated quality tests.*

· *The use of a public cloud[2] infrastructure allows the rapid deployment of an isolated test environment as soon as the continuous integration pipeline is triggered. This is also true for a local infrastructure where you can control the deployment.*

· *To ensure consistent replicability, destroy the entire environment as soon as testing is complete. This will also reduce infrastructure costs. However, be careful to keep the application execution logs for debugging purposes.*

· *Whenever possible, use exactly the same tools and deployment platforms for testing and production. Do everything, absolutely everything, "as code".*

---

[1] https://martinfowler.com/bliki/TestDouble.html

[2] AWS, Google Cloud, Microsoft Azure…

14

A soothing light illuminated the floor. There was the usual agitation of an end of day. As he walked through the collaborative space, Louis was amused by what he saw. The first time he had approached Denis' team he had felt like a stranger. But Louis, who didn't consider himself very technically competent, now knew how to differentiate between a performance testing tool, an automated test script, and an excerpt from an execution log on the screens of the employees. He had made progress!

As he walked through the room, Louis greeted the familiar faces who then looked up from their screens.

Hearing the footsteps walking towards him, Denis turned around and exclaimed: "I thought I recognized your voice! What brings you here?"

"Hi Denis, I've come to bother you a little. I need your advice."

"Tell me everything."

"I don't think I'm keeping track of the correct things. Since we've been doing automated testing, I feel that I don't have precise indicators of the effectiveness of what we're doing, nor do I know if we're making progress in our practice. I feel it, but I can't quantify it. The indicators I used in my previous experiences don't seem appropriate today."

"Which ones?"

"For instance, I was measuring the number of existing test cases, the progress of the test campaign, and the percentage of successful tests. I also measured the number of executions. It doesn't make much sense anymore. We run all the tests several times a day, so the number of executions becomes astronomical and it doesn't really provide any information."

Louis had concentrated his efforts to allow his team to focus on test automation. He had set up Fridays dedicated to practices improvement, established transparency on the group's progress, convinced them to redistribute certain responsibilities within the team, and even obtained a developer to support his group of testers. These were really great advances, but Denis realized that he had not taken the time to explain to Louis how to monitor and measure the improvement of their practice.

"What information do you want to get," Denis asked.

"I think I need to know the number of tests we have, and the success rate of the tests, and I don't know what else."

"These are clues, indicators," Denis said, "but it's not the fundamental information you want to know."

"I'm not following you…"

"Well, you want to cover three themes. Let's summarize. First, you want to know the health of the product you're testing and communicate this information to the developers. Second, you want to know if your tests are well written. And finally, you want to know if you are making progress in your automation practice."

"Yes, that's exactly it. Keep going."

"Okay, let's work together to establish the indicators that will allow you to track these themes. First and foremost, the first important indicator is the compliance rate of the product you're testing. That's something you already know and that will tell you what percentage of User Stories have their acceptance criteria validated. Each time you run the suite of your tests, you're able to give a snapshot of the product."

"This one is easy. We were already doing this with manual testing."

"What you can also add as a second indicator is the identification of fragile elements. During your test runs, you will be able to determine which modules and features are most prone to regressions. And this will be very useful for developers since they will be able to be more vigilant when they have to touch these components on the one hand, and on the other hand to focus their refactoring efforts where it is most needed..."

"...to reduce technology debt," Louis added. "Is there anything else that should be given to developers?"

"Yes, one last important indicator. They should be able to measure it themselves, but you could track over iterations their propensity to deliver bugs."

"They are not there to deliver bugs," quipped Louis, "but rather features."

"You're right, and yet they deliver bugs! If you were able to give them the number of bugs created per thousand lines of code, they would have important information. And if they follow this indicator they will see the effects of improvements in their practices."

Louis had a good understanding of these three indicators: a snapshot with the compliance measure, a trend with the identification of risk elements, and a measure of the maturity of the development practice to enable continuous improvement. Louis took note of these three points on his computer.

Denis continued:
"The second theme you want to address concerns your practice: are you doing things correctly? To answer this question you first need to define what you want to do."
"Well, automated tests!"
"No, more precisely you want to do Continuous Testing. You could measure its characteristics, but there are many of them and you would get lost in it. So I suggest that you set up four notable indicators."
Denis looked in his computer for a study on Continuous Testing produced by a key market player. He explained to him the basis of the study:
"You see, this study proposes to measure the results and not what we produce. We know that you have to have independent tests between them. But it's difficult to evaluate. However, it is possible to measure the consequences associated with this good practice. That's what this study is about."
Denis outlined the four indicators. The first: since it is impossible to have a high success rate with unstable tests, monitoring this rate therefore makes it possible to observe the quality of the tests. On

this point, Denis suggested setting a target of over ninety percent.

"Over the last thirty days we are at seventy-six percent," commented Louis. "We can probably improve on that."

The second indicator targeted the average time taken to complete a test.

"This is particularly relevant for tests done in browsers or mobile devices. The study shows that a test needs to be completed in less than two minutes to be twice as likely to be successful. So you should aim for an average of one hundred and twenty seconds or less."

"Do you know what our average is today," asked Louis?

"Yes: you're at two minutes and twelve seconds. That's good, your tests usually seem atomic, otherwise your average would be higher. You still have several tests that are too long. Follow this metric and make sure you improve it. This study focuses on tests done in web browsers, but the principle remains valid for tests on APIs. For these, take a target of twenty seconds including the response time of the application. We know that test environments do not always perform well, but this should be sufficient. Now: the third indicator. It concerns exclusively the variety of Web browsers or mobile devices used to do the tests."

"So I'm going to stop you right there. Our product is designed to run on a single browser. There's no point in testing it on other platforms."

"Make no mistake, first of all, because running its tests on several browsers requires a better design and will probably make them more robust. Secondly, we both know that web browsers are not forever. Who tells us that tomorrow the one that is your target is not going to disappear?"

Louis nodded. In fact, the joke of the moment was about an internal application designed to work only with Internet Explorer. When the HR software was implemented, the directive was that only this Web browser would be supported. A few years later, the Company had to pay a large price for the redesign of this software, which had become inaccessible to the new Apple workstations and the most recent Windows 10 workstations. This technological debt, a debt of portability, had been making developers laugh out loud for some time now.

"The last indicator is execution test concurrency," continued Denis. "Being able to run tests in parallel means that they are independent of each other. That means you have to manage your data well enough to be able to run multiple tests at the same time."

"How many tests do you think you need to be able to run simultaneously?"

"For tests using Selenium, at least as many as we have resources in our Selenium Grid. If you are able to make full use of it, then that will be fine. As far as testing on APIs is concerned, it's harder to put a precise number on it. The limiting factor is unclear. Will it be the processing capacity of the Jenkins scheduler agent or the load capacity of the application you're testing? It's hard to say. Try to find the right configuration that will give you the shortest possible overall execution time without overburdening your application."

Recently, Denis' team had helped them set up the execution parallelism. This allowed them to reduce the execution time of their test suite - which had become too large - from seven and a half hours to less than twelve minutes for nearly seven hundred test cases.

"On this point I think we are already on the right track," commented Louis.

"Ok. But be careful not to rest on your laurels. Some tests will become useless. Either because they never discover any anomalies, or because they concern very stable functionalities. Automation does not exclude the need for optimization."

"Yes, I guess we'll have to do some clean up. So let me summarize: success rate, average execution time, number of platforms, and parallelism rates. Okay, but why don't we measure coverage?"

"Because it will always be close to one hundred percent. Since you now test all the features in an automated way, there is almost no coverage issue, as there was with manual testing. In the past, time played against test teams and coverage was something that fluctuated with iterations. Now it's not a problem anymore, so this information is of little value."

The third theme concerned the improvement of the team itself.

"Once a month, I suggest that you monitor two indicators," Denis began. "At first, you should measure how well you respect the Dogma…"

"Dogma?"

"Yes, remember. You test, but only in an automated way, all that is necessary and sufficient to gain confidence in the product. It's very simple to see: just look at your timesheets."

In fact, the Company, like all companies, asked its employees to fill out timesheets every month. Each one had to distribute his working time over the different tasks referenced. Denis suggested to Louis to take advantage of this tool which seemed to interest only the accountants.

"You can be sure of one thing: everyone fills in their timesheets. All you have to do is calculate the ratio between the time spent doing automated tests and the time spent on all testing activities in general. In the first count, you have to include everything: scripting, maintenance, analysis, test data management, absolutely everything, as long as it is related to the automated test. The more you do 'only automated testing', the closer this ratio will be to one."

"But today there's nothing that differentiates all tasks," Louis replied.

"Your Scrum Master, or your project manager, will have no trouble using labels in your task tracking tool. It's pretty easy and at the end of each month you'll be able to do the calculation with a simple formula. It's called the Test Automation Effort Ratio."

"I see. Sounds pretty simple to measure. I guess today we're not so bad because we've left the rest of the manual testing to the business analysts."

"Oh no, you must be counting everybody's time! Continuous Testing is a whole team affair, not just the problem of the testers."

"That's true. We need to eliminate as many manual tests as possible, no matter who is in charge. Do you think it's possible to reach a ratio of one?"

"Maybe in some exceptional cases, but I've never seen it. But you know, we have stated this as dogma. So you have to do everything you can to get close to it. The idea is to continually progress, to be perfect."

Denis came to the second indicator that could reflect the team's improvement. He presented Louis with a five-level competency scale. The first level described the characteristics of a great beginner in test automation, the last one that of an absolute expert. Each level detailed demonstrable skills and the autonomy required for different tasks. Examples of online training were associated with each level, serving as guides for improvement.

"You can offer your team the opportunity for self-assessment. It's pretty easy. Each individual is able to quickly position themselves in one of these levels. If they do the exercise regularly you will be able to measure the average of your team. What you want to see is their progress. It may only vary by a few hundredths of a point each month, but it should progress. At the very beginning your average was close to one, the basic level. Do the exercise today, it will give you an idea of your overall level of maturity."

"And we need to aim for five, the highest I guess."

"No way. Take a good look. Level five corresponds to an absolute expert. His skills include creating an automated test framework from a blank page. You don't need that. My team, with people like Vlad, does that."

"So what score should we aim for?"

"I don't have an absolute answer, it depends a lot on your context. I suggest you do the exercise regularly and see how much of a score is comfortable for you. A good team is often heterogeneous. It includes beginners who need to be trained and experienced people who coach them. It's all about balance and it's up to you to determine it."

TO REMEMBER

- *The essential indicators for development are:*
  - *Product compliance rate*
  - *Default probability by modules or functionalities*
  - *The evolution of the number of bugs produced per (thousands of) lines of code*
- *Continuous Testing Benchmark[1] indicators are:*
  - *The success rate of automated tests*
  - *The average duration of a test*
  - *The number of test platforms used (tests in browsers or on mobile devices)*
  - *The execution concurency rate*
- *The team's progress indicators are :*
  - *Test automation effort ratio[2]*
  - *The team's average score, following the self-assessment of each team member, based on a clear and well-argued scale.*
- *Continuous Testing is a team affair, not just the problem of the testers !*

---

[1] *Continuous Testing Benchmark*, SauceLabs, May 2019, https://bit.ly/2LNSWbp

[2] https://www.tests.vg/the-test-automation-effort-ratio/, July 2020

15

"Here's Mona!" greeted several members of the team, happy to see their former coach again.

Mona had left her place to Max. Her role as a coach had come to an end: she specialized in coaching beginners and it was now established that her favorite team had acquired a certain mastery in the practice of Continuous Testing. It had been several weeks since she had left them and she had not yet had the opportunity to visit them again.

They had learned a lot from her, but most of all, her kindness had given them confidence in themselves and their learning abilities. The questions came from all around: how was she, did she miss them, and what was the new team she was accompanying like?

"Oh, beginners! They must have been like us when you took us under your wing," Michelle laughed. "How are they doing with the source code manager? Do they already have some experience?"

"Oh, not all teams are the same," Mona replied. "You know, most of them had worked with Java and a source code manager before, so there's less to learn on that side. I still have to explain to them how to test their application, since none of them had done testing before. But the most important thing is that they are curious."

"We've come a long way, you know," says Michelle. "Especially since we've managed to make our tests very robust, and they've become very stable now!"

"And we've even added some new things," continued Steve. "We are able to do a complete membership path, including email verification."

The team had begun to adopt the practice of isolated testing by replacing systems external to its application with mocks, but there were still a number of tests to verify the integration of the systems. Recently a user interface was added to a product module, requiring the creation of an account. When it was created, a whole mechanism for verifying the address provided as a reference had to trigger a set of actions in the application. However, in order to do this, a confirmation e-mail was sent to the user, who had to click on a link within ten minutes to complete the procedure.

"You see," explained Steve, "we created a Java library, based on the model of those present in the framework. It offers simple methods that will retrieve the url in the email received. We then use it in the test script. The test is a bit long. It has to wait for the email to arrive and the delay is quite variable, but it is the only one to be so long. And then, with the execution parallelism, it's invisible in all our tests."

"I see that you want to keep your tests as short as possible. That's good," nodded Mona. "Having a few that deviate from the rule is acceptable if you know exactly why you need them."

"Yes, and this is one of them," continued Steve.

Steve wanted to show Mona his library in more detail. As he got closer to her computer he started to explain how it worked. She listened with interest. Steve had been inspired by the different libraries existing in the framework, which were built to facilitate the life of the testers. He had taken their structures, philosophies and conventions. For the connection to the mailbox, he had opted for the use of Java libraries using the POP/IMAP protocol.

"At the beginning I had chosen to consult the mailbox using the webmail interface, but that posed some problems of robustness. Then I thought that with POP or IMAP, I would have fewer problems and this has been confirmed. Now, when our script performs the membership enroll path, it waits for the validation email, retrieves the link, uses it to confirm the address, and then finishes filling out the user profile!"

"It's a situation we find in many applications," commented Mona. "You should show it to Vlad, he could probably integrate it as an official module of the test framework for other teams to take advantage of it."

Steve didn't know Vladimir, Mona's colleague, well enough. Both were part of Denis' team, but Vladimir spent most of his time building the Company's test framework. Indeed, the number of initiatives integrating automated testing into their daily practice was constantly increasing and new technologies had to be integrated into the framework. Recently, for example, Vladimir was looking at the framework's ability to test mobile applications with Appium.

"Vlad will be happy to integrate it," she continued, "and it won't be the first time. For instance, the module that allows you to find test data just before executing the script originally came from a group like yours. We took it, improved it, and integrated it into the framework. It is now the central element of the test data management mechanism…"

Steve was both amazed to learn this and proud to imagine that his work could be of use to others. He was familiar with this data management module, and everyone on the team used it and found it devilishly useful. In fact, the essential information from the data present in the test environments had been centralized in a system managed by Denis' team. Very regularly, the information was updated to reflect the reality of what was available. The module made it possible to express in a simple way the logical characteristics of the data sought: type of customer, its characteristics, the products it was to hold, or the attributes of recent transactions. For the tester, it was very easy to express these needs using this simple language. The module then translated this into a computer query that queried the centralized database, found the appropriate datasets, and made them available for testing. Using this mechanism had greatly simplified the team's end-to-end testing; they no longer needed to maintain test data. The scripts took care of finding the appropriate datasets themselves just before the test was performed.

"Your module, if integrated into the framework, will probably simplify many situations for several of our colleagues," concluded Mona.

Mona, Steve, Michelle and the other members continued to share some news. The group was proud of its progress. With Max, they were beginning a new stage in their adventure. The automated test was bringing them significant value to the development team and everyone saw the importance they now had in the organization.

Mona was proud of them too. Everyone was committed to doing well, and some had followed Michelle's example by perfecting their Java skills. Many of them now had no difficulty understanding the technical discussions of their fellow developers, and they began to listen with interest. Through their learning, her fellow testers had managed to bridge an invisible gap between them and the developers, becoming one true team.

Before leaving the group, Mona showed Steve how to add his library to the framework's code repository. Finally, so that Vladimir could review and integrate it, Steve created a pull request. He had just made his first public contribution to the framework.

TO REMEMBER

· *The use of an open framework allows external contribution. You can design an in-house framework, while allowing inner-sourcing, i.e. contribution from teams within your organization. Open source frameworks, available on the internet, are also very relevant.*

· *In the case of inner-sourcing, the contribution must be as simple as for a public project: allow developers to create branches on your code repository and make pull-requests.*

· *Ideally, create anchor points (hooks) in your framework, offering structured interfaces for creating modules or extensions.*

· *Welcome the contribution as great news: it means that your framework is being used and that its users think it deserves to be enriched.*

· *Like any quality product, have a high level of requirements for your framework. It would be a shame, for example, if your automated testing framework were to be... little tested !*

16

"How long have you been working together?" asked Louis' wife.

"He's been bothering me almost every day for a year now," Denis joked. "Do you want me to get you a refill?"

Denis and his husband had invited Louis and his wife to dinner. This evening had forced the couple to do a little organizational gymnastics: pick up their two daughters from school, drop them off at their grandparents' house, and then drive downtown. But nothing would have prevented them from sharing a meal with their friends.

Before dinner, Louis and Denis had promised not to monopolize the evening with work discussions. So far they had held out. The appetizers and a good part of the meal had taken place without the subject coming up in conversation. But the temptation was too strong. Louis' curiosity outweighed his promise. And finally, he gave in.

"Speaking of bothering you," Louis continued, "I saw that you shared the quarterly statistics on automated testing."

"Indeed," Denis amused himself. "Are you going to ask me which group is following you closely?"

"Yes, do you know them?"

"Of course I do."

Denis deliberately left his friend unanswered.

"Come on, you know I want to know more!"

"It's a project that started more than two years ago. At the time, they wanted to get into automated testing. We started to help them, but they didn't listen to us. They decided to go another way. The results were questionable."

"How so?"

"It was a fiasco. For two years they searched for the best tool, wrote down several strategies and defined roles without worrying about the skills of their testers. In the end, they never found anyone capable of executing their plans. Until a few months ago they had almost no automated testing. When they saw your progress, I think they felt they were on the wrong track. They came back to my group for help with their testing practice. Mona has been with them for several weeks. And as you can see, the results are there."

"They're on our heels," acknowledged Louis. "We mustn't rest on our laurels if we want to stay ahead."

Until now, few groups in the Company had reached the level of Louis' team. Knowing that they were now in competition motivated them to always improve. Management was also looking at the numbers, and the managers were proud when theirs were at the top of the chart.

The meal was over. As everyone prepared to go out on the terrace to enjoy the coolness of the evening, Louis called out to Denis.

"I'm a bit frustrated right now. Some would like me to share my experience with other teams to help them in their transformation. I'm happy to assist them, but the problem is that I don't have enough staff to respond to all the requests. In addition, I must continue to deliver our initiative."

"I know very well who you are talking about. They also came to me for coaching," answered Denis. "But the problem is that there is no one to coach. They don't have a team of testers."

"Yes I agree. I made the same observation. So I offered them my help in interviewing the candidates. It was very difficult."

Louis explained to Denis the many problems he had encountered during this exercise. First of all, the lack of technical knowledge of some candidates had marked him. Then he had encountered the problem of the technologies used by the applicants. For many of them a refresher course was necessary, for others there was no question of changing tools. Finally, the last problem arose when a candidate had mastered the challenges of automation. He questioned the team's operating choices as if there was only one way to automate the tests, and no other way that he could see, regardless of the Company's context. Louis, who now had more perspective, had warned his colleagues.

"In short," Louis summarized. "In total, we looked at thirty-six resumes and recruited only one candidate with a good level of expertise."

"That's because you looked for experts. You should have looked for beginners."

"But if we recruit beginners," replied Louis, "we'll have to train them. Since they'll be on their initiative and we'll be on ours, we'll have to share our time. And you know it's very complicated. And I'm not even talking about the work we'll have to do to understand the functional aspects of their initiative!"

The spouses of Denis and Louis had settled on the terrace of the apartment. Located on the seventeenth floor, it offered a breathtaking view of the city lights. Soon they were going to be able to admire the last fireworks of the summer festival. The two friends continued to chat in the living room.

"You have reached such a level of maturity that you can now integrate beginners..."

"...and once trained send them to the other teams?"

"No, it is your experts that you will send to other teams. Sooner or later they will want to take on new challenges. So it's better for you to support them in their departure by helping them develop their careers rather than doing it without your input."

"But if I separate myself from all my experts, I won't be able to get by."

"Yes, but if you only send beginners," Denis replied. "They're not going to make it. The idea is to have balanced teams everywhere. You're going to send experts, but they're still going to have to recruit beginners, like you did when you started. However, you mustn't let too much expertise go to waste. To do this you can rely on the maturity index of your team. Try to stay above a minimum level in which you are comfortable. Make simulations by removing members of your group. If your level of maturity becomes too low then it is not the right time, or not the right person. But if you don't do anything and it's too high then maybe your experts will get bored, or risk stepping on each other. It's a matter of dosage."

"Yes, you're right. In fact, Michelle told me that she would like to start a project from scratch."

"Well, you see, she might be the first one to start on another initiative. Assess the level of maturity of your team without her and see how comfortable you are. You shouldn't let someone go if your level drops too low. Otherwise you put your initiative at risk."

"If I understand you well, I do what we did at the beginning but more gradually. I hire beginners to replace my experts who go to other groups to spread the practice of automated testing."

"That's it! And there is a positive side effect to that. Almost everyone will have the same practices. Either they will have gone through your group or they will have been trained by the experts who were in your group. So they're going to form a kind of community. They will use the same tools, they will share common concerns, and their exchanges will help consolidate their expertise."

They were about to embark on a new debate when fireworks outside intensified. They rushed to the terrace to see the end of the show.

Denis' husband saw them and called out: "You're just in time for the grand finale!"

TO REMEMBER

· *Often, publishing objective statistics will allow teams to compare themselves and stimulate healthy competition.*

· *Scalling Continuous Testing throughout the organization will require you to organize staff movements between your teams.*

· *Employees who gain experience will end up getting bored if they don't get new challenges. You can empower them by, for example, having them implement automation in new initiatives.*

· *Sharing the same practices across a company has many advantages. It is difficult to set up communities of practice when no common practice exists. It is easier when the community is made up of members who know each other, have worked together and collaborate daily to solve their problems.*

17

The hall of the convention center they had rented was packed to capacity. Its two hundred seats were insufficient, forcing many testers and other software engineering professionals to stand. Everyone was watching Jane's presentation, who had come from New York especially for the occasion. She and several guest speakers that day were participating in an event that was new to the Company: an internal conference on automated testing. Denis and his team had felt that there was now an audience and sufficient interest for this type of event. The employees' enthusiasm had clearly exceeded their expectations: the number of registrants to attend had quickly quadrupled. They had to find a bigger venue. Despite the three rooms allocated by the convention center, space was lacking.

The conference program was designed to cover as many topics as possible in one day. Concurrent sessions had been set up, adapted to each person's level and interests: there was a tutorial for beginners with Selenium, while a more advanced topic targeted people already comfortable with test automation.

Jane made the trip, as did half a dozen other guests, all experts in the field of automated testing and used to sharing their knowledge. At the end of her general session, questions about the different approaches to analyzing and optimizing the selection of automated test cases to be run were asked throughout the room. The very classy new-yorker responded with enthusiasm. After these exchanges, Denis announced the continuation of the program.

"As a closure for the day, we will present the feedback from Louis' team," he said, taking his place on the stage.

The conference featured the company's internal presenters: Vlad, the framework architect, had provided the tutorial for beginners using the internal framework, Mona had held an interactive session on atomic and independent scripting, and Denis had brought Louis into the feedback session in the form of a public interview.

It was a dirty trick Denis had done there to his friend and colleague Louis. He knew how easily Louis stressed when he had to speak in public. Louis, although worried, had not been able to refuse the proposal. They had worked well in advance of this presentation, their goal being to get the important messages across in a clear and concise manner.

Then came the time for questions. They were numerous, so great was the curiosity. They revolved around the various difficulties and explorations they had experienced and, of course, their results. Several groups in the early days of test automation were discovering colleagues they could rely on for advice and experience. Louis's team proved itself by responding directly to some of the questions from the audience, with Michelle taking the lead as usual.

As the day drew to a close, Denis thanked the various speakers, the enthusiasm of the participants, as well as all the people who had made the event possible. But before inviting everyone to the closing cocktail he announced the arrival of a surprise speaker.

Domineke, the Company's big boss, entered the crowded room. Although known to all, few had had the opportunity to meet or talk to him. A certain fervor came over the audience. Domineke, cheerful and dynamic, was a charismatic and respected character. He came to tell his experience about the testing in general and the automated test in particular.

"I'm a tester before I'm a CEO," he began. "Almost forty years ago, I started my career as a developer and then a tester. So, like you, I know how essential testing is in software production. I don't think we can neglect it. If it has been in the past, you and I will make sure it is not in the future.

We create softwares that allow us to do business. It is because we have control over our softwares that we can win new business. We are able to make them evolve quickly, in line with market developments. But we can't do that without quality. And if it is possible, it is thanks to you.

As you know, our markets are in constant transformation and this is accelerating. All of us, you, me, are being asked to move faster and faster. This is why we have decided to introduce the DevOps practice in our software department. You have certainly heard us talking about continuous integration, continuous deployment. Well, we have adopted a shift towards the Cloud. Automation is what will allow us to move faster. Too often, testing remains manual. Since we can't do it manually any faster, nor can we neglect quality, it seems essential to me that we massively and systematically adopt automated testing in our practices. Testing can no longer be the missing link in our automation processes. If anyone in the Company tomorrow tells you that we don't have the time or the budget for it, that's bullshit. Send them to me! I'll make it my business to personally remind him or her how, today, automated testing is no longer an option."

TO REMEMBER

· Communities of practice are also created around events - community events. Internal conferences are ideal for taking a step back, weaving human networks and discovering each other's stories and experiences.

· External experiences are also valuable. Many professionals willingly share their knowledge. Invite them to your events: sharing is often altruistic.

· The public demonstration of support from your governing bodies is an extremely powerful source of motivation.

18

"It's a classy pool. Did you have it built or was it here when you bought?"

"It was here. It was a big factor in convincing us to buy this house. The girls love it. Your husband also loves it, he's still paddling!"

"Denis, Louis... Would you like a refill?"

"The same thing, that would be perfect."

"Yes, the same thing. Thank you, my darling!"

"Okay, so a punch for Denis and a beer for you."

"You're missing a bar and a barbecue by the pool. The kitchen is far away..."

"Yes, it's in our plans. But we'll install it next summer. There aren't many days left to enjoy the pool, so the investment can wait a little longer..."

"Daddy, look!"

"Yes my darling, I see you! Bravo! Don't you swim anymore, Denis?"

"No, the punch suits me very well for the moment. Let the children enjoy the water. And then you'd probably try to sink me, unsuccessfully."

"Haha, you're right. I'd probably try and I'd surely fail."

"You're bitter! You're still mad at me about the conference. But it wasn't so bad and you did well."

"Yes, but you know how uncomfortable I am with public speaking. But it's true, I found it pleasant. That name, though - OktoberTest."

"It was cool, really cool, as a name for a conference like that. I don't see what you're blaming it for. Besides, I think we touched a lot of people. Remember that tester who came to see us at the cocktail party at the end of the day?"

"Yes, he told us that he felt that the practice of the test was finally being considered. It's true, and a great point. But still, it was a dirty trick to get me into it. I'll get back at you."

"Not by drowning me anyway, you recognized your incompetence in that field."

"I did. Listen, I wanted to propose something."

"Ah, what else have you invented? Go ahead, tell me."

"I was thinking we could write a book to tell this whole story."

"A book? Definitely! You're hiding your dirty tricks well, aren't you?"

"Hey, you didn't expect that, did you? But think about it, I'm sure it could be useful to others. Thank you darling for the drinks. Anything I can do to help?"

"No, no, it's okay. Drink fast, you only have ten minutes to remake the world, no more! Girls, let's eat soon!"

"So what do you think? Shall we do it?"

"I'm telling you, it's a dirty trick! But okay, we'll do it. I don't know where this is going, but let's do it."

"Haha, I was sure you'd like the idea. We'll discuss it after vacay, okay?"

"Hell no! Don't expect to get away with that: we start tomorrow."

"Tomorrow? Shit, what have I gotten myself into again?"

"It was your idea, admit it!"

"I admit it, I admit it. Well, everyone's out of the water, looks like they're hungry. Time to eat!"

Valentin Guerlesquin is a software engineering professional. For more than ten years he has specialized in software testing. He has held various roles within several organizations, including test environment management, manual testing, application performance evaluation, test data management and of course test automation. Valentin is certified ISTQB Full Advanced and TMMi Professional. Very committed to sharing and improvement, he has participated in training several of his peers in many organizations.

Henri Bigot has been an IT professional for nearly fifteen years. He is dedicated to team management and achieving ambitious goals. He strongly believes in the value of people, rather than tools or processes. Today, he leads an enthusiastic team of software test developers. During his career, Henri has created rich and varied opportunities for himself. He has worked in Europe, Asia, and North America, where he has been able to immerse himself in different cultures.

© 2021

ISBN 9798714903359

Thanks to the reviewers Grégory, Brigitte and Pascal for their time and their wise remarks.